ONE SUCH AS ME?

Pioneering Spiritual Mental Health Support

Marja Bergen

ONE SUCH AS ME?
Pioneering Mental Health Support

Photography by Marja Bergen.
Cover design by Wes Bergen

Marja Bergen
www.marjabergen.com

For Wes,
my loving husband and friend,
faithful through
thick and thin

THANK YOU!

CONTENTS

FOREWORD

Marja Bergen's life has been difficult and continues to be so as she tries to improve conditions for those who, like her, live with mental health challenges. But it has been an extremely meaningful life too.

It is doubtful that she could have seen what lay ahead of her when she first began her fight against the stigma of mental illness in 1993. She seemed oblivious to how she might be risking her own reputation by the openness with which she spoke about her mental health challenges.

It is then that Marja heard God's clear call to raise mental health awareness among Christians, knowing that there are none better equipped than those people who know God's love and know how to share that love with others.

She saw the great injustice of the shame attached to mental illnesses that sufferers were helpless to prevent, something that sadly was especially evident in churches. With her own story and actions, she decided to demonstrate that there is no need for such feelings of shame.

Through extensive speaking and writing, she set about trying to change the misunderstanding that so many had about mental health. Revealing her experiences with bipolar disorder did not take a great amount of courage on her part, since the child she had inside her trusted that she was doing God's work and that He was with her in that work. With enthusiasm and passion, she told her audiences about how God had worked in her life.

Despite her health problems and despite the stigma that would follow, Marja would not let anything stand in her way of answering God's call on her life. Her desire to serve continued throughout her ups and downs, no matter how painful the battles became. At those times when she found it necessary to draw back, it did not take long for her to come back with renewed effort, since God was at her back. She believed without doubt that by trusting her heavenly Father, His will would be done. And she felt deeply inspired to be His hands and feet.

God made a rich life possible for Marja, especially during those years when she helped churches, and their congregations, gain better acceptance and understanding of people with emotional disabilities like her own. The amount she accomplished as a single person is a testament to how great and powerful is the God we serve. Indeed, her life shows how God can turn weakness into strength. In reading the pages ahead, you will be blessed as you learn how God loves every one of us, whether we are healthy or ill.

Harold G. Koenig, M.D., M.H.Sc.
Professor of Psychiatry and Behavioral Sciences
Associate Professor of Medicine
Duke University Medical Center, Durham, North Carolina
Adjunct Professor, Department of Medicine, King Abdulaziz University, Jeddah, Saudi Arabia
Visiting Professor, Shiraz University of Medical Sciences, Shiraz, Iran
Editor-in-Chief, *International Journal of Psychiatry in Medicine*

INTRODUCTION

I've been looking forward to telling this story for a very long time. As I write this, I'm 78 years old and I really do need to get down to it before I'm no longer able. My story will cover the most important parts of my life, the period between the years 2000 and 2014 when I raised mental health awareness in the Christian Church.

This is God's story, with me only his foot soldier, a person who gave her all to his work, despite great struggles with the symptoms of bipolar disorder. God gave me the courage and the strength to do something that I had not heard of before—speaking to Christians about faith and its relationship to mental health.

The most important part of this work included the founding of Living Room in 2006. This story describes my passion for it and how God helped me develop it into a major ministry that was spreading far and wide. Living Room groups provided a place of refuge for those who were at the time being shamed out of their churches. The groups encouraged participants in their faith. Jesus and his love became a major source of their healing.

I worked hard to help Christians and their churches understand what it meant to live with mental health challenges. They started to develop compassion and learned to treat people like me with greater acceptance and love. Through extensive writing and speaking, God helped me prepare the soil for those who would follow after me.

I had wonderful moral support from my pastor and from my Brentwood Park Alliance Church family, but my ability to meet all the demands on me—leading my group, speaking and writing, and giving support to individuals in crisis—proved to be too much for a person with challenges like mine. I and my church did not have the resources to continue the broader ministry of planting more groups.

In 2014, I was relieved to have Sanctuary Mental Health Ministries merge with the Living Room ministry. I hoped that Living Room would have a better future with them. Tears of regret flowed over having to let it go. Living room had been my calling, a vibrant ministry since 2006, but there had been no indication that help would be forthcoming. I felt guilty for not being able to continue.

Four years later, in 2018, much to my dismay, Sanctuary dropped Living Room as part of its mandate. The ministry I had worked so hard for was abandoned. It was not until this happened that I came to realize the extreme importance of the peer support that Living Room had offered.

It has been proven, and I know from experience, that there is no support as effective as the kind of support people can give to those who share similar needs. Christian peer support groups are vitally important. There are few other places where individuals with mental illness can gather to talk about both: their emotional struggles and their trust in God. Those who don't have lived experience can't hope to empathize in the way peers can.

The loss of Living Room has meant that Christians are learning "about" what mental health challenges are, but the voices of those who experience it have disappeared, along with their groups. We are talked "about," as though we're "victims," set apart from the "well" people who are being equipped to support us.

At Living Room we were supported by our peers, all of whom had lived experience. We came to realize that faith in God could help us overcome our challenges. Within our groups we had no one looking down on us or talking "about" us. Through Jesus and his love, we were able to encourage each other to be more confident. We learned that we could be "victors," despite our challenges.

This book will help you in your struggles with challenges. I hope it will remind you that you too can be victors when you trust God and remember the healing love of his son, Jesus. I hope you will be inspired by my story—the story of one of your peers.

This book will also be helpful if you don't have mental health challenges but want to make the world a better place for your Christian brothers and sisters who live with such challenges. It will give you a window into the heart and soul of a person who lives with bipolar disorder but is doing her best to build acceptance and compassion for people like herself.

During the period covered by this book, I had my journal with me almost constantly. Because I wrote in it whenever a thought or happening occurred, the book includes a great amount of detail. I also drew from a weblog that I started in 2006 and from emails that I kept. Thus, much of what you'll read is in the present tense—described as my life was unfolding.

I hope you'll enjoy travelling with me as I take you through this most exciting time of my life. And I hope you'll be inspired when you read how much God can accomplish through a person when she's dedicated to God, despite great challenges.

May God bless you all.
marja

CHAPTER ONE

DEVELOPING SELF-ESTEEM
1965 - 1988

IF YOU CAN KEEP YOUR HEAD . . .

It was 1965. I was nineteen years old, a student at Simon Fraser University, when my life became chaotic.

I suspected there had been something strange going on with my mind for months—thoughts and experiences I wasn't able to understand. I was confused, couldn't make sense of what was happening around me or within me. Found myself doing bizarre things I couldn't help.

A series of old Shirley Temple movies was run on TV at the time and, because I had always loved her, I believed they were being played especially for me. I watched each one. Patiently, but squirming, unable to sit still.

I imagined a radio show in a foreign language was broadcast with special messages for me. Falsely believed that I could understand what was being said. These are the kinds of tricks my mind was playing. I was extremely frightened by it all. When my distress was at its worst I banged my head against a wall in an effort to stop the torment.

I got worse. When my screaming had become unbearable, my parents called a cab and took me to the hospital. In the emergency room I shouted obscenities at the staff, something much out of character for a person who had always been quiet and reserved. They gave me a sedative to try and settle me down.

A doctor came and talked to me. He noticed the poetry book I had brought along. Leafing through the pages, he found *If*, by Rudyard Kipling and asked me to read it out loud for him. I read slowly as the sedative was taking effect, absorbing every word.

If you can keep your head when all about you
Are losing theirs and blaming it on you,
If you can trust yourself when all men doubt you,
But make allowance for their doubting too.

It was as though the words were written especially for me, as though Kipling had known that a person like me would need to hear those words one day.

Each line I read held meaning, and as I slowly began losing consciousness, hope rose within me. I finished reading the entire poem before falling asleep—always to remember the effect its inspiring messages had on me. Despite the terror I had experienced, the poem helped me see that there was hope.

I had felt alone in a terror-filled world, but that doctor made me feel that someone cared. He gave more than simple medical treatment could. Through the poem, he gave me the courage to carry on.

The poem travelled with me through the rest of my life. I read it often or listened to it on Roger Whittaker's album as a Song for Erik. I've often been reminded of the words and they always held a lot of meaning for me.

When I found myself lost in thought, as I so often was, I remembered:

If you can dream—and not make dreams your master.
If you can think—and not make thoughts your aim.

And then I would get up and start baking something or begin work on a project I'd been considering.

During painful times, I was moved by the powerful challenge:

If you can bear to hear the truth you've spoken
Twisted by knaves to make a trap for fools,
Or watch the things you gave your life to, broken,
And stoop and build 'em up with worn-out tools:

I don't believe this doctor had any idea of how positively my life would be impacted by what he did for me. I have often wished I could thank him for so wisely having me read this poem during such a critical time.

He did not just see me as a deranged young person. He saw me as someone who needed care and empathy.

There are many ways in which a person in crisis can be helped. It takes a calm approach by a caring caregiver who understands that the distraught person they see in front of them is only going through a temporary crisis. A person who simply needs time, some good medical care, and compassion.

There's a story from the Bible about a man whose sufferings were somewhat like mine.

> *"When Jesus got out of the boat, a man with an impure spirit came from the tombs to meet him. This man lived in the tombs, and no one could bind him anymore, not even with a chain. For he had often been chained hand and foot, but he tore the chains apart and broke the irons on his feet. No one was strong enough to subdue him. Night and day among the tombs and in the hills he would cry out and cut himself with stones."* (Mark 5:2-5)

This wild, crazed man was believed by all the townspeople to be possessed by demons, a condition often confused with mental illness. But Jesus cared for the man, not judging him by what ailed him but seeing the man for the person he was. He was not afraid of him but drew close and commanded the demons to leave him. Jesus healed him as he had healed others.

In the past, uneducated people considered mentally ill individuals to be spiritually unwell, or "not right with God." This was a dangerous diagnosis to give to otherwise God-loving people. Those living with mental illness have bona-fide medical conditions beyond their control yet are left feeling shame, thought badly of by their community. The damaging effect on their lives can have enormous proportions, often leading to hopelessness that makes ending their life preferable to the emotional pain they experience.

People like this tortured man were often considered evil. But I believe much greater evil is committed when a sane man treats such a person unkindly or in a hurtful way. Are we doing that?

The man was greatly relieved when Jesus freed him from the turmoil that had possessed him. He begged Jesus to let him follow him. But Jesus, who so often said *"Follow me"*, now said, *"Go home to your own people and tell them how much the Lord has done for you, and how he has had mercy on you."* (vs 19)

So the man went away and began to tell in the Decapolis how much Jesus had done for him. And all the people were amazed. (vs 20)

This homeless, crazed, bleeding and frightening man made a valuable contribution to Jesus' ministry. He became one of the best witnesses possible—one who had suffered greatly but found healing. If this is possible for a person such as him, what's possible for us?

Although I didn't believe in God when I first got sick, I believe he was there in the wisdom and kindness of the doctor. And Jesus would one day send me out to testify to others about him, in the way he sent the man he had healed out to testify about him. I would tell others about him and his love, and what he could do in our lives.

And that's what I did. And with God's help, that's what I'm doing now.

KINDNESS REMEMBERED

When I woke up, I found myself in a ward with many empty beds. I was the only one there. Looking at the chart on the nightstand, I learned that I was at Crease Clinic—part of Riverview Mental Hospital, an institution most commonly referred to as Essondale at the time. This place had a bad reputation. In fact, it was the object of many cruel jokes. I pulled the covers over my head, hiding myself, and went back to sleep.

When the staff woke me up, I found myself in dreary surroundings with all kinds of people that differed from any I had known before in my sheltered life. They were not like the friends I had been used to spending time with. Although I was surrounded by fellow patients, I felt quite alone.

This was a most depressing place. It would be a place where there would be no privacy. No quiet place I could call my own.

One morning I was pacing the hospital hallway, not connecting with the world around me, as was often the case in those days. My mind was a place of confusion. My psychiatrist, Dr. McDougall, having just come into work, drew up beside me. Warmly putting his arm over my shoulder, he cheerfully asked, "And how's my friend today?"

How wonderful that word, "friend," sounded in this place where I had been feeling like such an alien. Where all the other patients were older than me. A place where nothing seemed normal.

13

Have you ever thought of the significance of that word? Have you ever been in a bad place, a scary place, a place where darkness fills your mind, and have a kind person call you a friend?

I've come to see that a friend is a person who will accept you, though you might not be at your best. A friend is a person who will show you they care when you're going through a hard time. A friend will listen carefully and try to understand you. A friend is a person who will share their inner selves with you, in the way you do with them. To have a friend is to know you belong.

Dr. Gerald McDougall was that kind of person for me. He did not tower over me like some doctors might. One day, he pulled a picture from his wallet and showed me his family, in the way a friend would. He made me feel like a real person.

This kind doctor came to walk with me through some of my toughest years. It would not be until many years later that I had another psychiatrist like him—someone who treated me with dignity, someone who cared about me.

Years later, when my baby was born in a difficult delivery, Dr. McDougall carefully watched over me, visiting several times during my hospital stay. He made sure I was well taken care of, even arranging for someone to sit with me when I was going through a rough time.

When Dr. McDougall left to take a position in another city, he called me personally to let me know. As I fought back the tears, he asked me to send him a card at Christmas. I did that, and I did much more. I wrote him often to keep him up on how I was doing, glad when I was able to send him good reports.

Upon his retirement I received another personal call from him, asking what I would like him to do with all my correspondence. I told him he could throw it away. He gave me a phone number where I could reach him if needed. Unfortunately, I wrote it on a scrap of paper which I never found again. How I kicked myself!

Dr. McDougall treated me with respect. He showed that he truly cared. I was made to feel that my life mattered. I was treated as a person of worth.

How fortunate I was to start my life as a mental patient being so well treated. I felt this doctor's love.

Although I would not come to believe in God until some twenty years later, God knew me and my needs. And even then, he was looking out for me.

A SPECIAL KIND OF MAN

I spent three months at Riverview, was discharged, and readmitted a few months later. During the intervening time I met Wes, the person who would be my partner for the rest of my life.

I met Wes during a most difficult time. He must have liked me, although even then I talked up a storm—something he has a hard time dealing with today. He was truly special, sticking with me when I spent another six months in hospital. Who else would have done such a thing?

When I started getting weekend passes, Wes spent Saturdays and Sundays with me. He loved his Triumph sports car, so we spent a lot of time going for drives. There were a couple of occasions when he took me where we would be around other people. In those days the medications were not like today's and patients were frequently over-medicated. As a result, it was often obvious that they were mental patients. That was true for me too. But Wes did not show any shame about being seen with me.

Wes spent a lot of time in our family's home on those weekends. And on Sunday nights he joined us to have the fried chicken dinner my mother always prepared. After dinner came the drive back to the hospital. Always a bit late arriving back, we had to bang hard on the heavy metal door to be let back in. My heart would sink to know I had another week in this dreary place.

Two or three years after my discharge from hospital, when I was doing much better, we were driving on Hastings Street in Vancouver when I mentioned to Wes, "So, when do you think we should get married?" A proposal wasn't needed. We both knew that we were meant to spend our life together. We started planning.

May 3, 1969, was our wedding day. It wasn't an expensive affair. We saved our money for something more important— the honeymoon. So, the day after the wedding, we flew to London to begin a five week road trip through Europe, seeing as much as we could in that time. It was the first of many trips we would take—to many different places.

I can't tell you enough about what my relationship with Wes has done for me. His steadfastness gave me a sense of security. Sharing our photography hobby became a big part of our marriage and gave us something we had in common. He was patient with me when I became difficult, trusting that I would not always be like that. Loving me nevertheless.

How might my life have turned out if I didn't have Wes at my side for those many years of marriage we have behind us today? I can't imagine it. How was it possible for a person like him to stick with me all these years? A person with my history. A person with my many problems.

Only One could have done all this for me. Although Wes didn't have a faith, I believe that God, through his great love, worked through this man's kindness to me. And today I can see he had a plan for my life all along.

Looking back as I am on this day in 2024, I am seeing how big a part God was playing in my life, long before I knew him. And when I came to believe in him and trusted him, I started to allow him to lead me. I started following Jesus, trying to be like him—to be his hands and voice and feet. I grew into the kind of person God could use.

MY PHOTOGRAPHY

In 1969, a few months after Wes and I came back from our honeymoon, we joined the 65-member Lions Gate Camera Club. It soon became a big part of our life together. With the help of fellow members, as well as accomplished photographers who came as guests, we learned how to create good photographs. I came to love the creative outlet it gave me and worked hard to take the best pictures I could.

Wes and I spent many of our years together searching for good places to photograph—from our own garden to city parks, to national parks, and even to countries abroad. Our focus was always on finding good things to take pictures of. Bringing back good images gave us something to share with others at the club.

Photography was a way of expressing what was inside me. It encouraged me to look out at the world around me and appreciate the things I saw in a way I wouldn't if I weren't always looking for the "perfect" picture. Young children were my favorite subjects. Following children around and capturing them being themselves gave me a lot of joy.

The club was a place where I could share with others in the love of the hobby. It was a good social outlet. I always had people with whom I could join in conversation about our common interest. When I had an award-winning picture I received praise that made me feel good about myself.

During my first fifteen years at the club, I still suffered much from my mental condition. I was still on Chlorpromazine, the one medication the hospital had prescribed for me, not yet taking other medications that had been developed. It was sometimes obvious that I had mental health challenges. Despite that, I found myself fitting in quite well. I was as one with them.

In later years, I did some professional photography, freelancing for the Burnaby Now Community Newspaper for a couple of years. I was also commissioned at times to do candid photography of young children in their home environment. I had one-person gallery showings. Most of the work I did had a focus on people, probably my most favorite theme ever.

When my mobility issues made it hard to get down to the low level needed to best photograph small children, I started photographing the flowers we brought into our home. I also liked to keep an eye on the oft-changing sky and catch the interesting things that developed where too many people forget to look.

The three people we've talked about—the emergency room doctor, the psychiatrist in the hospital, and Wes, my husband were instrumental in helping me build my confidence. But, as you can see in the story I've told you about my photography hobby, we don't have to wait for such support to enter our lives. The confidence I built depended to a large degree on myself and the kind of life I came to build for myself.

There are so many choices of creative outlets in the world. If everyone with struggles like mine were to try some of these they would learn to build their self-esteem and might very well discover a life filled with meaning. If you're reading this and wondering what could be possible for you, you might surprise yourself. All it takes is the courage to try.

Photography was something I enjoyed so much that I wanted to work hard to do well at it. This did a great deal to develop a positive self-image in me.

I started out very small, taking dozens of pictures of ducks at Stanley Park while I was learning to use my camera. Gradually I discovered the kinds of subjects that later became my favorites. I used many rolls of film before my pictures started showing promise.

Rudyard Kipling's words often came to mind:

> *If you can dream—and not make dreams your master;*
> *If you can think—and not make thoughts your aim.*

Remembering those lines motivated me to stop dreaming about things but to get moving and act. Doing so paid off in many ways.

As my life went on, I ended up with a lot of different creative projects. They gave me a sense of fulfillment. And, after I became a Christian, my work was able to serve God in many ways. Through him, I came to develop a positive view of myself.

I LEARN TO LEAD

Lions Gate Camera Club met every Thursday night and each night of the month was devoted to some activity—slide and print competitions, workshop, showcase, or a nature competition. A chairman hosted each of these meetings.

Soon after we joined, Wes started showing himself to be a leader by chairing various of these nights. In the friendly atmosphere of the club, I felt comfortable joining him by being co-chairman, helping out at slide nights and print nights.

As the years went by, I became more courageous, gradually taking on more responsibilities. I came to chair a variety of the club's meeting nights. As print chairman, for example, I would host evenings once a month where members brought the best of the 16 x 20 enlargements they had made in their own darkrooms. They competed for the gold, silver, and bronze awards chosen by guest judges.

I enjoyed the task of finding guests who could add to our knowledge and inspire innovative approaches to our photography. In all the leadership roles I held for the club, including being president for a year, the belief I held was that we needed to be challenged to grow in the art form. I felt that it was too easy for a group like ours to become ingrown in its work. We needed to be aware of what was happening outside the club.

The most difficult part of chairing meetings was having to get up in front of everyone to welcome them and to introduce guests. This was very difficult for me. In fact, while serving various roles for the club, including being president for a year, I don't think I ever got completely over the nervousness.

Despite the problems with speaking, I managed to join in with the rest of the leadership of the club along the path it had taken from when it was first founded. The only thing I needed to lead, was the willingness to do so. No one judged me to see if I would be trustworthy in a position. And when I took on a job, I was ready to commit to it. I was aware of the mental health crises I sometimes faced, but having such challenges did not hold me back from doing all I could.

During my first fifteen years as a member of the Lions Gate Camera Club I lived with much depression, and even occasional psychosis, able to hide it most of the time. I'm sure that this must have shown in my behavior at times, but I don't recall talking about it or bringing attention to it. As far as I knew, it wasn't discussed by others either.

Around 1988 or so, I started receiving more effective medications and my mental health improved. Was it a coincidence that this happened around the same time when I was developing my faith in God? Both the medical care and spiritual growth proved to be the ingredients I most needed to help me gain stability.

At the club I was respected for the work I did in photography and for how I carried out my responsibilities in the roles I took on. Nothing else mattered.

The many years of varied work I did during my serious involvement with the club, provided me with confidence and a good foundation for the leadership skills I would later need to make a difference in the lives of people with mental health challenges.

CHAPTER TWO

MEETING GOD
1986 – 2004

MEETING GOD, MY FATHER

Around age 40 or 42, I was still experiencing the occasional psychotic episodes that had first put me into hospital at the age of nineteen. When they occurred, I suffered greatly. The one medication I had been on from the beginning, was not managing my bipolar disorder nearly enough. There was no denying that I needed more help than the medication could provide. In my mind I struggled:

Could I have been wrong all these years to deny the God who everyone had tried to tell me about? Could this God help me? I felt his pull.

Yet I wasn't ready to try church or to get help from people I knew to be Christians. Instead, I went to the public library to learn more. I found a little book (I believe it was Are You There God?) that talked about God, and I surprised myself, able to agree with everything it said. I began to realize how I had been wrong all those years to deny this God who is greater than myself. Would he be able to help me with my suffering?

Before this, I had often lain awake at night, wondering about him, but could only manage the conclusion that God must be "the force that drives nature." I could not imagine him being someone who might have a personal interest in me. I could not have imagined the kind of love he had to offer. Not until I became emotionally broken, did I truly meet him. Even then, it took a while before he became real to me. It took a while before I felt his love enter into that deepest place, my heart.

But here I think I need to tell you a little more about myself. We're all different and the way in which we need God in our life will differ somewhat from the needs others might have. God meets us in the kind of person we've grown to be and the kinds of needs we have. He knows us better than we know ourselves.

And me? I am a child. I always have been and probably always will be. I know it from how I feel about things. My feelings tend to be unfiltered. My tendency seems to be to look at the world with the innocence and clarity of one who is seeing the world and the people in it for the first time.

When I look upon a tulip covered with raindrops, the best part for me is not the flower, but the "tears." It's the feelings of things and of people—of what's in my heart that matters most. I believe my feelings best reflect who I am. They're at the root of what God made me to be. A child from the beginning.

I've often thought of how accepting God was for me like being a child, playing a game with her earthly father. I stood with my back to him while he stood a short distance away, encouraging me to trust him. When he gave the word, I fearfully allowed myself to fall backwards, not completely able to trust that he would catch my fall.

In a similar fashion, I came to trust my Father God. Somewhat fearfully at first. But spiritually I let myself fall backwards, not completely sure that he would catch my fall. But God, my Father, caught me safely in his arms. And I found the peace that trust in an almighty Father can provide.

Children have an innocence, making it easier for them to be trusting. The child in me eventually learned to trust God and his son Jesus fully. Once I had made my decision for him, my heart was wide open to receive him. From the beginning, I started experiencing him in my heart. I developed an intimacy with Jesus that has proved to be precious to me and has helped me share him and his love with others.

God blessed me with the eagerness of a child and I longed to serve. But later in life, I think it might have helped if I'd had more qualities of a grown-up. More reservation about sharing myself so freely. And yet, it's my nature to be sincere and honest, and it's that Marja I bring to this book to share with you.

What helped me as I was becoming a follower of Christ, was to realize that having God living inside me meant to have his love there. God and love are synonymous. They belong together. One night I asked God to fill my heart with that love. It didn't take much more than that prayer to have love's warm feelings enter. Something definitely happened inside me. One thing I found was that God's love is not mine to hold tightly and keep to myself. It's meant to be shared. With God's love inside me, it wasn't hard to love others.

When I read my Bible I learned so much more, absorbing the wonderful truths it showed. I learned how Jesus, God's son, gave himself for us. How he died and how my sins are forgiven through what he did. Jesus became real to me. Truly mine. I became transformed.

I STARTED GOING TO CHURCH

When one of the Pharisees invited Jesus to have dinner with him, he went to the Pharisee's house and reclined at the table. A woman in that town who lived a sinful life learned that Jesus was eating at the Pharisee's house, so she came there with an alabaster jar of perfume. As she stood behind him at his feet weeping, she began to wet his feet with her tears. Then she wiped them with her hair, kissed them and poured perfume on them. (Luke 7:36-38)

As I was developing my faith in God, I joined three friends who were attending Cliff Avenue United Church. I thought I'd try that church, since my friends seemed to like it. I respected these ladies, especially since they hadn't tried to pressure me, or tried to "save me," which I would have had trouble with.

My first time at the church happened to be Easter Sunday, something I hadn't expected. As a result of being so very detached from religious practises, I had forgotten about Easter. For years it had only been about chocolate and Easter eggs for me. And so, being at church on this particular Sunday came as a bit of surprise to me.

On this occasion there was a performance by a semi-professional children's group with wonderful music. I was overwhelmed by it all and broke down in tears. I didn't know where those tears were coming from but could not hold them back. Deeply embarrassed, I wished there was a way to leave, but I was sitting near the front. Walking to the back to leave the church would have made my tears doubly obvious.

Despite the tears, I kept being drawn back, eventually becoming a regular attendee. I remember the many tears I wept on Sundays when I first became a believer. The tears just happened, without apparent reason. A friend even led me from the sanctuary one time so I could cry in private, releasing my pent-up emotions.

As I remember this, my thoughts go to the woman who washed Jesus's feet with her tears, as described in the Scripture above. How well I can identify! I wrote about it in a devotional long ago:

Her tears tumbled down like the tears of a child. In the greatest expression of gratitude, one that she didn't plan and couldn't have helped, tears spilled over Jesus' feet as he was reclining. With love, and in an act of worship, she wiped his feet with her long hair. She kissed them and poured perfume over them. For so long she had been without care or guidance, lost in a world that didn't care about her as a person.

Not long after, I joined a Bible study group, eager to learn all I could about God and about Jesus. Years ago, I wrote about how I felt, identifying with the enthusiastic Mary as she sat at Jesus' feet, listening to him. (Luke 10:38-39)

This teacher was different from any other person she had known. He spoke in a way she hadn't heard before. He was wise, though humble. He revealed truth to Mary's hungry heart. By current standards, he was a radical, showing compassion for the sick and befriending those who were considered outcasts. He spoke about a heavenly kingdom, one that she would not have to wait for, but one that had already arrived.

Yes. I had been hungry without realizing it. God was filling the emptiness I'd had in my heart for a long time.

I was a regular member of the study group for as long as I attended this church. Those meetings were probably more important to me than almost anything else. I wanted to know all I could about the Bible and I loved discussing what we learned.

Being part of this small group, opening our hearts to each other, built intimate relationships that became precious to me. Through the friends I developed in this group God was connecting with me in a very real way.

MY SEARCH FOR MEANING

Back in my mid-twenties, when I had been married for a short time and had only been out of the hospital for three or four years. My emotional state was extremely unstable. I suffered much with depression, mania, and psychosis. And I was under stress much of the time. Psychiatry was still a relatively new medical field and the medication available to me at the time was not very effective.

I had tried working at an office full-time but soon had to switch to morning hours only. Although Wes and I only had a one-bedroom apartment, I found housework overwhelming. This was especially so since I had told myself that if I had to cook every day, I would look on it as an enjoyable time and make it my hobby. I tried out many different recipes. It all took a lot of time. My ironing sat for weeks before I had the motivation to work on it.

Nevertheless, I ended up with enough free hours during which I worked on needlework projects. This provided me with the glorious quiet alone times that I needed.

In my book A Firm Place to Stand I recall those precious hours spent in solitude (Pages 189 – 191)

> Those afternoons gave me important hours to think about what I wanted out of life and what I wanted to give to my life. I did a lot of inner talking, especially on the countless occasions when I felt sorry for myself, thinking of the great difficulties I faced. And when my ruminating mind threatened to bring on the paralysis of depression, I remembered Rudyard Kipling's line: "If you can think – and not make thoughts your aim." I learned to be a doer.

As I worked, I thought endlessly of what was important in life and how I would like to use my time. I decided to give instead of take; I wanted to make instead of use. The conclusion I reached was that after I died, I wanted the world to be a better place because I had lived. I felt a need to leave something of myself behind. 'Yes', I thought, 'I will create heirlooms, beautiful things to leave to my children, a record that I have lived and accomplished something. I intend to live a life of value. Life is too precious to waste. While I'm able, I must use my days as well as I can.'

And so my thoughts went, day after day. I encouraged myself, became angry with myself, struggled to hang on, tried to come to terms with the stigma. And I filled my time working with colorful yarns and embroidery cotton. Whenever a low mood began to descend, I tried to ward it off with a new project.

I cross-stitched a large Dutch sampler with very fine stitches. In the center, I embroidered my initials and in the lower right corner, my name, and the year it was made. My son and daughter-in-law will receive this after I die. It would be one way of leaving something beautiful behind, a little piece of my history, one way to prove that I have lived.

I made a needlepoint version of Millet's famous painting, The Gleaners. I made petit point portraits of native children. I taxed my eyes creating single-thread petit point roses to mount in small oval pendants. I undertook the huge task of crocheting a wool Afghan in Afghan stitch and then covering it with an intricate cross-stitched flower design. It became a wedding present for my son and his wife.

All this work was fulfilling; it was comforting. But throughout, I struggled with my emotional balance. I had to work very hard to stay in control and to live the kind of life Kipling had prescribed for his son, even when I sometimes watched ". . . the things I gave my life to broken" and had to ". . . stoop and build'em up with worn-out tools."

Throughout these years, the poet's words buoyed me up, "If you can fill the unforgiving minute with sixty seconds worth of distance run – yours is the Earth and everything that's in it, and – which is more – you'll be a Man, my son!" His advice was fatherly. He understood true difficulties. He understood me.

To lead a life with meaning, we need to know that what we do and what we are matters. We need to know that there's a reason for living. My search for meaning led me to create material items. It was all that was emotionally within my reach in those early years of my adult life. Going beyond this to a more mature view of life's purpose took years.

But at this time in my mid-twenties, I certainly learned how to treat my life as a treasure, one I did not want to waste. What Lord Chesterfield said became how I lived: "Know the true value of time; snatch, seize and enjoy every moment of it. No idleness, no laziness, no procrastination; never put off till tomorrow what you can do today."

With so many wonderful projects to fill my time, each day became one I looked forward to. I gradually learned to believe more in myself and began the slow process of building self-esteem.

MY SEARCH FOR FAME AND FORTUNE

I loved photographing young children at their most natural. Feeling a bit like a child myself, I could relate to them. But using the pictures for camera club competitions was not enough. I wanted to see my pictures published. Many of them were good editorial material. I did find several markets in the U.S. and was able to sell many. To see my pictures serve a useful purpose was satisfying.

Nevertheless, I wanted to earn more than the little I was receiving for editorial purposes. I yearned for some kind of tangible proof that my work had value. I wanted proof of my own self worth. My photography was more than a hobby; it was of ultimate importance to me. Unable to have a full-time job, I felt the need to be recognized for something.

I wanted to gain a reputation for my photography. For that to occur I needed to get my work out there to be seen. When the United Nations Year of the Child was happening in 1979, I saw it as an excellent opportunity to have an exhibition of child photography. I showed my work to the curator of a small gallery. To my delight, she accepted my proposal for a show. The exhibit was publicized in several publications. In addition, a cable television station produced a fifteen-minute documentary about my work. With that, I was on my way. Other one person shows followed.

I was receiving the recognition I had hoped for. But it wasn't as satisfying as I thought it would be. Gradually, I no longer considered it so important to be famous.

All my creative work had taught me that doing my best was of utmost importance if I was going to be satisfied with myself. The more I gave myself to my work, the more pleasure it gave me. Producing photographs for club competitions trained me to seek perfection. When working in my darkroom, I worked hard to get the perfect print. Many rejects ended up in the garbage can before I was happy with the results. I learned perseverance, something that followed me in other pursuits.

When I freelanced for a local community newspaper, I spent a good deal of time at each assignment. Even after I had taken many pictures at an event, I hated to leave, thinking that I might miss something important. I made every effort I could to produce the very best photo story possible. Long after other photojournalists had gone home, I was still there, watching, waiting, and recording.

This patient kind of approach to my work helped me as I photographed children at a dance competition, capturing their nervous excitement as they waited for their turn to go onstage. The photos were published as a spread in the paper and resulted in an offer from the BC Festival of the Arts to be their official photographer in 1988.

It was such an honor to be asked, and yet I could not commit myself to something that big. The festival was months away and I could not foresee how my health would be. I've lost many such opportunities, at that time of my life unable to count on my stability.

But although I was being very productive, I felt as though nothing was enough. Time and again I asked myself, 'Is that all there is?' The things I did seemed to lack sufficient purpose. I was never satisfied. Not until after I had turned to God was I able to inject meaning into my work by using it to minister to people in various ways. Only then did I find sufficient reasons to publish my photos for others to see. In later years, they became part of the Reflections on God's Word, which I started sending out in 2013 to give spiritual support for readers' mental health needs.

Once I found God and my spiritual journey had begun, my outlook on life quickly changed. My new discovery of how God loved me and how he had a purpose for my life, thrilled me. I felt called to follow Jesus' example.

I learned from Bible readings how God wanted me to love others as he loved me. During my morning prayers, I often asked God to fill me with his love and to help me share it with others. God answered those prayers. All I had to do was ask. Jesus said that it is more blessed to give than to receive. (Acts 20:35) I found that to be very true. More than at any other time, I felt God's love as it flowed through me when sharing it with others.

Eventually, God's love led me to a life I could never have imagined possible in my earlier years as a Christian. Jesus gave me opportunities to serve God and to be there for others instead of myself alone.

I made an important discovery. Heirlooms made of cloth and yarn do not compare to caring for those around me. I didn't have to do anything grand. I didn't have to be famous or make a lot of money. Keeping Christ's love in my heart as I spend time with others and work for their welfare is enough.

AS CHILDREN OF A CREATIVE MASTER

Living a creative life has infused a spirit of joyous enthusiasm in me. It came from hearing God's frequent urgings within me to the possibilities of making good things happen. Beautiful things. Things that are needed by others or are useful to them.

I've tried my hand at many creative pursuits: knitting and crocheting, needlepoint and petit point, and cross stitch. But writing and photography have been my greatest passion. They allow me to bring what's in my heart to the surface for people to see.

I once responded to Psalm 23 when my small group was studying it, saying: "I don't want to lie down in green pastures. I want to make things happen." Today I realize that we also need to find peace as we spend time with him, resting from our busyness. And yet . . . .

I believe life is a lot more interesting and exciting when we make things happen instead of simply watching. More often than not, God is calling us to join him in contributing good things to the world, in big ways or in small ways. The trouble is that so many choose not to obey God's call, listening more to their own will—their own desires.

Don't think that making good things happen always involves work. Often, the most important work we do feels more like play, especially if it's something God has uniquely gifted us for.

Being creative is to be attentive to what we see in the world around us. It's bringing color into a life that might otherwise be no more than a gray existence.

Think about this:

As creators, we are like our Master Creator himself, making things that never existed before—doing things that would never have happened if it hadn't been for us. Even with the smallest item we create, we could be leaving the world a better place because we have lived.

Our reward is a feeling of wholeness, knowing that our life is meaningful and that we have made a contribution.

I believe that the best creative arts are not preconceived, but arrived at by a process of exploration and discovery as we follow God's promptings and guidance. I've already talked about my photography but would like to say more in terms of it as a creative effort.

In my photography, I seldom plan exactly how I'll be composing the pictures I work on. When I want to photograph an amaryllis flower, I make many exposures. I never take only one. I explore, looking at the flower from all sides—from the top, looking down on it, from underneath, looking up. Moving in close or further away. Trying different backgrounds. I use windowlight that is forever changing the flower's appearance, depending on the weather and the time of day. There are always new opportunities.

The time will come when the flower starts to wilt. This does not have to mean the end of my exploration. It means that there are further opportunities for my heart to find expression. I often photograph a flower until there's little left of it, sometimes taking a hundred exposures of a single flower. It's so wonderful that we're able to do that nowadays, no longer having to think about the cost of film and processing.

I believe that photography is not about "taking" pictures. It's about "making" them.

When I think of God our Father and how he made the earth and everything in it, my imagination suggests that he might not have preconceived what would come out of his work either. It might have been a process of discovery for him as he poured out his love, bringing it to the surface, layer upon layer for all to enjoy.

The Bible says that "God saw all that he had made, and it was very good." (Genesis 1: 31. That indicates to me that he was pleasantly surprised as he stood back to see what he had done. Can you imagine what the Garden of Eden must have looked like to him as the result of the lavish love he had poured into it?

If you are someone who, like me, enjoys the creative arts, can you see how what's in your heart shows through your work? And isn't that sharing of your heart where most of the satisfaction comes from? And don't you too sometimes stand back to look at what you've done and wonder where it all came from?

I believe it came from our Father God, our Master Creator, who frees us to let go of what's in our heart and let the world see it. Because what we honestly bring forth from our heart matters.

And for those of you who would like to paint, or photograph, or write, or sculpt, or anything you'd like to try your hand at, God can help. He can help you find the confidence to do so when you trust him to help you let go and discover what you have inside you, sharing it with others through your handiwork.

Let God release you from what might be holding you back. Discover the freedom to flourish—to blossom, to be whole and complete.

"MY YOKE IS EASY"

Jesus revealed himself to me at a time when I had great needs. Matthew 11:28-30 spoke powerfully to me and I listened eagerly. How I needed to hear those words!

"Come to me, all you who are weary and burdened, and I will give you rest. Take my yoke upon you and learn from me, for I am gentle and humble in heart, and you will find rest for your souls. For my yoke is easy and my burden is light."

This invitation from Jesus gave me great comfort when I was beginning my journey with him. I had been stressed out by illness, trying to cope with it on my own but failing. My world was chaotic. I so needed peace! How welcoming it was then to read these words and to know I didn't have to be alone with the struggles anymore—to be offered rest from the strain that I had lived under! While I was weary, feeling lost and needing more than the world could offer, Jesus himself humbly bent down to me and called me to himself.

With my youthful spirit of those early years of my faith, I accepted his call, responding with joyful obedience. I could do nothing less. He had captured my heart.

Jesus' invitation to accept his yoke lit a flame within me, a desire to learn from him, a desire to join him in the work he was doing in the world. Jesus promised the work wouldn't be heavy. He promised to be right beside me to help me carry it. I wanted to serve and needed rest for my soul as well. Jesus assured me I would have both.

What does Jesus expect from us?

He wants us to take his "yoke" upon us. A yoke is a wooden contraption that is placed over the shoulders of two oxen so that they can pull a weight. In Jewish teaching a yoke represents the obligations a person must take upon himself.

As a rabbi, Jesus was a radical, bringing a new interpretation of Scripture and a revolutionary kind of thinking. To take on

Jesus' yoke is to follow his way of thinking and to follow his example and teachings. Jesus' call is a call to discipleship, a call to follow him and learn from him. To accept the obligations he places on us. Yes, Jesus places a burden on us. But he helps us to carry it and it is lighter than the burden sin lays upon us.

It has been many years since Jesus' words from Matthew spoke to me in such a strong and clear way. But they dug themselves deep into my heart and mind during a critical time of growth. Today, the words may not necessarily come to mind, but I have been living according to their message, through good times and bad. They have helped shape me into who I am today, a person who loves to share Christ's encouragement with those who need him.

I know it's wonderful because I've been on such a journey. The road is not always smooth. In fact, it can be extremely rough at times. We might suffer, but when we serve, there's joy in that suffering. I could not imagine a more meaningful life.

I am reminded of the Fireside Chat I gave in July 2006 at Sacred Space, a New Age boutique in Vancouver. Isabella Mori, a mental health advocate, had invited me to speak about how my faith helped me with my mental illness. She said it would be an interview, with me responding to her questions. Such an opportunity!

My pastor at the time, impressed the importance of this talk on me by quoting Romans 10:14-15.

> "How, then, can they call on the one they have not believed in? And how can they believe in the one of whom they have not heard? And how can they hear without someone preaching to them? And how can anyone preach unless they are sent? As it is written: "How beautiful are the feet of those who bring good news!"

Besides Isabella and a friend and me, there were five others in attendance. When the time came to begin, Isabella introduced me and then . . . she just invited me to begin talking! It didn't turn out to be an interview after all! What should I do? I didn't have anything prepared.

Fortunately, I had my Bible with me and Matthew 11:28-30 came easily to mind. I read the verses and spoke freely and eagerly about what coming to Christ and following him had meant to me. No hesitation. I was in love with the Jesus the verses spoke about, grateful for how he had given me rest from the struggles I faced. The talk went well.

I thanked God for giving me the courage to speak.

FREEDOM TO BE ME

Do you remember what it was like to be a child, exploring a new playground? Everything new. So much equipment to try out that you'd never seen before! That's what Cliff Avenue Church was like for me as the new Christian I was. My years in that church, starting in 1986 or 88, must have been among the happiest of my life.

I imagine I was quite a sight to behold as I lived out my joy and my enthusiasm at Cliff. Forever eager, not tiring, as I played out every idea that God put into my head. Transforming ideas into action— "Not making dreams my master, nor making thoughts my aim," as I followed Rudyard Kipling's teachings.

Under the leadership of Pastor Dale Cuming, Cliff was like a playground might be to an overactive child with unlimited opportunities for creative involvement in church life.

I took part in a ministry that visited members of the church who could no longer attend because of illness or old age. It was a joy to create booklets for them at Easter and Christmas. The booklets included a message from the pastor, and a wide variety of items that a shut-in might need to help them deal with their isolation: uplifting thoughts and stories to warm their heart, items to help remind them of good things in their past, short pieces that would help them smile, words to familiar hymns they could sing to themselves, and prayers. Each booklet was illustrated, usually by a young person from the church. Work parties folded and stapled them, adhering a photograph to the cover.

On behalf of the Cliff congregation, I organized the publication of a cookbook. Almost everyone in the church got involved. 28 businesses in the community helped sponsor the project with donations to help with the printing. We were able to collect many great recipes from this congregation where everyone loved to cook and bake. At the launch, we had a luncheon featuring foods for recipes included in the book. It was a special affair, kicking off a very successful fundraising campaign.

It was wonderful to be given a bulletin board in a corner of the foyer that I could use in any way I wished to express my joy and my faith in God. It was my effort to inspire the same in those who might have a look at it. I used Scripture and photographs, some of them showing church events that had taken place. I had the same heart that I would have in 2013, for putting together devotionals and sending them out.

I kept busy like this during all my years as a member of this church, only slowing down during times of depression, which I remember were sometimes pretty severe. But upon recovery, I carried on as though nothing had happened.

I myself am baffled at how I did so much and where my many ideas came from. I loved it all and found myself much encouraged by my church family. Looking back today, I recognize how I had been loved by those around me! How very kind everyone was. Strange how it's only now, as I tell you my story, that I'm fully realizing it.

These activities showed the pleasure I took, and would always take, in serving God in multiple ways, wherever my heart might be moving me. While at Cliff, my attention turned to mental health. This is where I was when God's call first came to advocate for people with mental health challenges. In everything I did, I believe that the needs I saw in people's lives were what most motivated me.

God has given me many gifts to help me serve him. And how wonderful it was for Cliff Avenue Church to give me so many opportunities to use those gifts! I am very thankful to have had this church as my "playground."

CHAPTER THREE

A MENTAL HEALTH ADVOCATE
1993 – 2005

NO ONE BROUGHT ME FLOWERS

Cliff Avenue Church became the training ground for how I would serve God in bigger ways later on. This was my church home in 1993 when I first decided to come out in an effort to reduce the stigma of mental illness.

I had read an article in a mental health newsletter by Dr. John Varsamis who said, "If everyone with a mood disorder would tell a close friend or family member about it, and educate them, there would soon be no more stigma." That inspired me.

I found the whole stigma thing very ugly, causing people with conditions they couldn't help to be rejected by society. If there were no stigma, they wouldn't have to deal with such feelings of shame.

I decided that the best way to beat it would be to show that I myself am not ashamed of who I am. I would educate by telling my story. If I wanted things to be different, it would have to start with me.

I sent an article to *the Vancouver Sun*. Editors wasted no time publishing *Sick, but No One Brought me Flowers*, together with my name and picture. The article described what it was like to be nineteen years old and a patient at Riverview Hospital. The moment I arrived at church the next Sunday, my friends there surrounded me with big hugs. They were proud of me. What wonderful memories those are!

Not long after, I began work on my first full-length book, *Riding the Roller Coaster* which was published in 1999. That book will require a story of its own. I will tell you about that later.

Everyone in my world knew. But coming out did not hurt me very much. I didn't care if there were some people who thought I might be weird. For the most part, I didn't think they did. I had many friends and felt I had their respect, even if they did know that I had a serious mental illness. I felt good about myself and learned to walk with confidence in all areas of my life.

The book gave me credibility and so, the church was a hundred percent behind me when I proposed a depression seminar. We had two. One took place in the year 2000 and another one in 2001. Members of the church trusted me fully to organize these events. The church felt proud to be offering this unique opportunity for people to get help for their emotional needs in a church environment.

These seminars were among the first occasions when mental health was addressed as a topic that Christians and their churches needed to hear about. The speakers at the first seminar were Dr. Roy Bell, lead pastor of First Baptist Church and psychiatrist, Dr. Fred Adrian. They were pioneers in bringing the topic of mental health to churches. Throughout the seminar they took turns, one talking about the medical side of depression, the other speaking about the spiritual side of things.

The keynote speaker for the next year's seminar, was Dr. Phil Long who spoke in the morning. The seminar was well attended. After a beautiful lunch, prepared by the women of the church, the people who had gathered split into two groups with a facilitator for each. One group shared what it was like to live with depression, while the other group provided a space where caregivers could share their experiences.

In a most innocent way, I moved forward, for fourteen years joyfully doing what I felt God leading me to do, speaking out to build mental health awareness. I fully sensed the importance of what I was doing but was blind to how the reality of stigma might affect me. Years later when I found myself stigmatized, I wondered at times whether I should have been so open. But I was never sorry I did.

Would my life have been easier if I hadn't come out in the way I did? Probably. I had no idea at first how much suffering it would cause. But if I hadn't done so, my life would not have been nearly as meaningful as it turned out to be. I was following Jesus and helping people with mental health challenges have better lives. And that was important to me.

Why didn't I feel ashamed about being so open? Coming out was definitely a sacrifice I made, though it didn't feel like it. People were calling me courageous, though I didn't feel courageous. I simply did not feel there was anything to be ashamed of. And this was the message I acted out.

RIDING THE ROLLER COASTER

A few years after the Vancouver Sun article was published, I started to think about the needs of those who, like me, lived with mental illnesses. I'd had a productive life, despite my nine months in a mental hospital when I was younger. I wanted to encourage others with struggles like mine, by writing about what I had learned about coping and thriving.

I considered the many who were being diagnosed with a mental illness and how they would be affected by what the world thinks of them. I thought of what this unjust stigma might mean to them and their outlook on life. And, having thus far led a good life myself, I wanted to let them know that having a mental illness does not have to mean the end of the world. A satisfying life is possible.

And so, not too long after my 1993 article in the Vancouver Sun had appeared, I started writing *Riding the Roller Coaster*, a book that would be published in 1999 by Northstone publishing (now Wood Lake Books). This, my first full length book on mental health, was a cross over book, suitable for the secular and Christian markets. It wasn't long after this that I recognized the importance of building understanding in the Church. I believed the Church was the best place to find the love of God. People with mental illness hunger for that kind of love.

Today, as I write this in 2024, I recognize the book's significance in a way I didn't at the time I wrote it. It was highly unusual at the time for people to make their mental illness publicly known. And it was possibly the first book written by a person openly discussing her struggles with such an illness while at the same time helping others with similar struggles. As a result, the book received a fair amount of attention.

Roller Coaster contains vignettes of what my life with the depression and mania of bipolar disorder was like. Interspersed are descriptions of the symptoms, and much encouragement. All the material was designed to help those who were affected take a positive spin on what life could offer them, despite their difficulties.

There are lists of how to cope: what to do when you don't feel like doing anything, when you can cope a little, and when you feel stronger. The lists were drawn up while I myself was learning how to feel better through my many ups and downs. I don't think I had seen coping techniques like this described before, certainly not from the perspective of a person who has personal understanding.

With this book, I proved how a person's experiences of illness can provide compassion and understanding of a kind that isn't available to those who have never lived with such struggles. For that reason, I believe it's a significant example of the importance of peer support. It's a biblical truth that *"we can comfort those in any trouble with the comfort we ourselves receive from God."* (2 Cor 1:4)

I wrote during a time when word processing programs were not yet in common use. So everything was written longhand, rewriting each page over and over until I had a copy I was happy with. I was very fortunate to have had the help of Robert Winram who was the Executive Director of the Mood Disorders Association of BC (MDA) at the time. Whenever I was unsure of what I had written, I faxed a copy to him and received much welcomed advice and guidance.

Despite my mental health struggles, I could not leave the writing alone. I kept my journal beside my bed, ready to immediately write down ideas when I awoke. I remember sitting on a hospital bed working on my writing, frustrated that I didn't have more time and a better working environment. But I was fortunate to have a kind psychiatrist while there.

Dr. Fred Adrian showed some interest in my writing. I felt like I must have had something in common with him when he told me about a little book he had just purchased by Henri Nouwen, an author who had inspired me greatly as well. What comfort it is when a person who shares your faith is looking after you!

I would meet Dr. Adrian again when the book was published and I was doing a reading at Chapters in Metrotown. He surprised me when he appeared and bought a book from me. I also connected with him when he was a presenter at the depression seminar I organized at Cliff Avenue Church not long after.

Northstone publishing was excited about the book. When it was ready, they provided a little launch via a conference call from their office with all their employees present. They had me read *Sick, But No One Brought me Flowers*, which I had included in the book and I heard the applause over the phone. I was told that tears were shed by some of those who listened. It was a good send-off.

I gave readings at the main branch of the Vancouver Public Library and other places, becoming known as a person willing to speak openly about mental health issues from a personal perspective.

In Victoria, Bruce Saunders of *Movie Monday* was excited about the book. Bruce was the person whose brainchild had been regular showings of films related to mental health issues at Victoria Mental Health Centre's Eric Martin Pavilion. He was a big support for me and sold many copies to his audiences.

One day Bruce invited me to come and speak to his audience, many of whom had bought the book. It was great to hear the responses readers offered. I was overwhelmed when one woman told us that she kept *Riding the Roller Coaster* on her bedside table, frequently reading portions of it. "It was like a Bible," she said.

In the Introduction to the book, I wrote:

> "Often I wondered what I was doing writing a book such as this. Was I qualified? But as so often happens with the hardships we endure, I was able to glean an understanding that I can now pass on to others."

I GREW SPIRITUALLY

Despite my good experiences, there came a time when I felt a need to leave Cliff Avenue, the church that had been my spiritual home for fourteen years. It was painful to leave this church family, the place where I had begun my Christian walk.

I went through a five-week grieving period. Every morning during those times of sadness, I put on Mario Lanza's *I'll Walk with God* album, and listened as I settled into my leather chair, cradling a cup of warm coffee in my hands.

> *I'll walk with God*
> *I'll take his hand*
> *I'll talk with God he'll understand*
> *I'll pray to him*
> *Each day to him.*

And I did pray, daily asking God to show me where to go next. And so it was in 2005 that I decided to try Brentwood Park Alliance Church. The church was close to our home. In fact, I used to walk through its parking lot whenever I took my son to school.

BPAC was an evangelical church, quite different from the mainline United Church I had grown accustomed to. But it was a better reflection of the faith environment I had grown up in as a child. The focus at this church was to spread the gospel beyond the walls of the building. I had never thought I would have a zeal for mission work. But with time, I surprised myself. I would find out that I had a lot I wanted to share.

I came to love the worship times with the lively songs, the keyboard, drums, guitar, and bass. The people were warm and friendly. This congregation was younger than the one I had left. At the Ladies' Bible Study I attended, I was one of the older members. I learned to feel at home with people of all ages.

When I first came to the church, I familiarized Pastor Don Dyck with what it meant to have bipolar disorder. I thought he should know about it. A time might come when I needed support from the church. I told him about how strong my moods could be. With my hand I described a slight up and down wave for how the average person experiences moods, and then I described the roller coaster fluctuations of moods I go through.

My pastor prayed with me, asking God to help him learn about bipolar disorder. And he did learn much about what I deal with. I often emailed him about things I was going through, and he came to know me and my disorder. I trusted him, in the way a child might trust a loving father.

I was brand new at BPAC, but from the time I gave my *Riding the Roller Coaster* book to the pastor and his sister to read, I was well supported by them. The book helped them recognize that mental illness needs to be addressed. They realized how people like me need friendship and support. And so, they gave me all they could.

Sermons at BPAC were 45 minutes long, much longer than the ones at Cliff were, but they fed me richly. The sermons showed how I could apply biblical teachings to my life. I listened eagerly as I heard messages of Christ's love and compassion. Today I can see how the devotionals I ended up writing years later were influenced by this pastor's teachings.

He brought the message home, not only through his sermons, but also through the way he lived, especially in his support for me.

Through Pastor Don's teachings, Jesus came alive for me. I grew spiritually.

MENTAL HEALTH RETREAT

In 2005/06 I was involved in the planning committee of a mental health retreat in Abbotsford, put on by the MCC Supportive Care Services (name later changed to Communitas). Keynote speaker for the event was Dr. John Toews, a Christian psychiatrist and author of *No Longer Alone: Mental Health and the Church*.

The weekend consisted of messages from Dr. Toews and break-out groups. There was plenty of free time as well. I was asked to speak to one of the groups but didn't have the courage to do so on my own. Someone shared the speaking with me. However, I later came to see that I would have done alright and I was sorry to have declined.

Two new friends from BPAC came to support me, though I didn't really see the necessity. I was puzzled by their presence. No one had ever supported me like this before. I felt cared about, made to feel special. One of them was to become the best friend I'd ever had.

The organizers were disappointed that the event did not draw clergy or other leaders to learn how their churches could effectively address mental health needs in their congregations. It was decided to hold Dr. Toews over for a few days to offer a workshop specifically for pastors. Very much wanting to help this to be a successful event, I offered to do the publicity for this and try to draw as many as I could to the event.

Though the retreat was still six months away. I was driven to begin work immediately. I wrote letters and articles and talked to those who needed to be informed. I also began writing my book, *A Firm Place to Stand*. My feelings were strong, I was inspired. It was a struggle to harness my moods and retain day-to-day control, yet I focused well on the publicity work. The issues were clear in my mind.

I worked hard to get the word out, wherever I could, in whatever ways I could. I sent emails to Christian organizations that ministered to clients with mental health issues. And I did not stop until I had done everything I could possibly think of.

Bipolar disorder brings a lot of trials with it, yet in her book, *Touched with Fire*, Kay Redfield Jamison, psychologist, and writer, identifies a number of positive qualities of hypomania and mania that people with the disorder experience. Amongst them are "fierce energy, high mood, and quick intelligence; a sense of the visionary and the grand; a restless and feverish temperament." That looked a bit like me. I suppose that the workshop I was promoting marked the beginning of the "visionary and the grand" qualities I would end up showing in my future work.

One of the diagnostic criteria for mania is "sharpened and unusually creative thinking and increased productivity." Although I don't often get manic, I believe that the way I work zealously at things is a product of my hypomanic (mildly high) tendencies, something that comes in quite useful when you're trying to get things done.

One of my favorite pieces of Scripture comes from Matthew 19:26 with Jesus speaking to his disciples: *"With man this is impossible, but with God all things are possible."* I have found that by trusting God, this became true in many of my endeavors. We can accomplish much when we're dedicated to serving him.

My publicity campaign proved to be successful. Two workshops were given. And though discussion about mental illness and the Church was not common at this time in history, the workshop drew sixty participants in Burnaby and a hundred in Abbotsford. I was delighted to see my new pastor and the associate pastor from BPAC in attendance. Frank Stirk, a Christian journalist, was also there, taking notes throughout the presentation.

Dr. Toews' core message: "The Christian faith can make an important contribution to mental well-being. But being Christian does not guarantee mental health." He taught the gathering about mental illnesses and the kind of support people with such illnesses need. Pastors and church leaders returned to their communities, better informed and better able to help those under their care.

This introduction to mental health care, as well as what he had learned from me, prepared my new pastor to hear about the needs I had identified for people with mental health problems. In 2006 he was open to hearing how I felt God leading me to form a faith-based support group for such people.

I WROTE ABOUT MENTAL HEALTH AND FAITH

Word about me as a person who could speak about mental health and faith issues started to spread. In 2005, shortly after joining the BPAC congregation, the Canadian Mental Health Association, BC Division (CMHA, BC Div) asked me to write about mental illness and the Church. This marked the beginning of work I would be doing—not only speaking to churches about mental health, but also speaking to secular audiences about the importance of faith to our well-being.

In 2005 I wrote *Mental Disorder: The Result of Sin?* And in November 2006, my online article, *The Church as Supporter* was published. I wrote:

There is a danger of approaching clergy who are not educated in the field of mental health. The true problem might not be recognized and much needed medical attention may be delayed. Pastor John Manlove of New Life Community Church in Burnaby recognizes this danger. "There are many churches and Christians who tend to spiritualize every problem and consider it unspiritual to seek help from a mental health professional. I would like to see more Christians mobilized and trained to give support to those struggling with mental illness." But there are even Christians who themselves experience mental health issues that assume their problems originate from spiritual shortcomings.

I was passionate about the role I felt Christians and their churches should have and used my blog to speak from my heart:

To have people who are supposedly following Christ, cause this shame is more hurtful to Christians than almost anything else imaginable. Christ did not teach us to be that way!! He taught us to love unconditionally. He loved the outcasts and the stigmatized of his day. *This* is how he teaches *us* to live as well. Christians have lost touch with Christ's teachings.

God has so much to offer us. The Bible has so much to encourage us and give us peace, despite our great struggles. Aside from the medicine the doctor gives me, there is nothing like my belief in a loving God to keep me well. There is nothing like a church family to help us keep this faith alive. The Church needs to find ways to *help* us with faith, instead of blaming us for not having it.

When a church friend or pastor tells us that there must be something wrong with our relationship with God, the results could be tragic. When a person who is already feeling the pain of depression is told that the fault lies within himself, nothing could be worse.

I had found wonderful support in my previous church and again at BPAC. And because it came from friends who shared my faith, it was better than support I received from other sources. Followers of Jesus can use his example and share his love by being non-judgmental and compassionate—qualities not always available in other segments of society. Such friends encourage those who suffer to cling to the knowledge that God is there, even if he doesn't seem to be.

God loves us through people. If we are Christians, we are called to be God's representatives. We need to represent him well.

When I started my blog, I came to hear from individuals who left the Church when they were made to feel ashamed about their mental health struggles. One person told me that she'd had no Christian support. Churches she attended had not been open to hearing about such problems. The pastor of one church knew of her illness but warned her not to let anyone in the congregation know about it. "They wouldn't understand." As a result, she had no Christian friends with whom she could be open about her problems. She spent three weeks in hospital not feeling she could tell anyone. No one from her church prayed for her or visited.

Bolstered by such stories, my motivation to reduce stigma remained strong. Though struggling much with stress, I could not—and never would—let go of the call God had on my life.

The nature of the call would change over the years, but my determination always remained to make the world a better place for people living with mental health challenges. In 2023, I would trust God in helping me put out the message that followers of Christ need to address the pain that's caused by stigma. It's a change of focus from where it was in 2006—going from reducing the stigma to healing the painful effects of stigma.

CHAPTER FOUR

DEVELOPING PEER SUPPORT
2006

MDA AND PEER SUPPORT

I don't believe that Living Room would have had the start it did if it didn't first have the example we found in the Mood Disorders Association of BC.

Through MDA I came to see the great value in peer support. Living Room became an outworking of the MDA model—people with mental health struggles helping others with similar struggles. Participants learning from each other, helping each other learn to cope. Learning that they're not alone.

The MDA of BC had its start in the recreation room of Vicki and Ed Rogers' Vancouver home in 1982. With Ed newly diagnosed with bipolar disorder, they saw a need to gather and share with others who were facing similar mental health challenges. The first meeting drew six to eight people.

Word spread and the group soon outgrew the basement of their home. Within six months they had to move their monthly meetings to Sunrise Community Hall in Vancouver. People came from all over the Lower Mainland to attend. When participants arrived, they were immediately made to feel welcome at the door. Coffee, tea, and cookies were always waiting for them.

From the beginning, it was understood that it was difficult for some to have the courage to come to a group like this. During group discussions, an effort was made to make people comfortable, aware that not everyone would want to be open about what they were dealing with. They were encouraged to just listen if that's all they felt up to doing.

Within those first six months of meeting, the group was offered a year of government funding that allowed them to have an office in Vancouver. It was hoped that they would, besides having meetings in Vancouver, spread the peer support model to other parts of BC. They became an association.

One day in early 2006, I was attending an MDA meeting when the facilitator went around the circle asking each of us to tell what their best way is to cope with symptoms. I knew that my best way was to go to God, to trust him, and to lean on him. But how would this secular group feel about me talking about God? I didn't want to make members of the group feel uncomfortable.

And, when I thought about it, Christians with mental health challenges did not feel comfortable discussing their issues in church groups. I started seeing that they needed to have a place of their own where they could talk about both—the difficulties of living with mental illness as well as the God who could help them cope.

That's how the idea of Living Room came about.

MDA became a great partner. They taught me how to facilitate. And I used their manual as a guide in preparing our Living Room Facilitator manual. They referred Christians who needed support to our groups.

It was a blessing to have such an enthusiastic partner in MDA. They loved what's happening with the Christian groups. It was a blessing to be connected with a secular organization that so fully supported a Christian ministry and encouraged the Christians amongst them to share their faith.

In 2017 MDA became part of Lookout Housing and Health Society.

GIVING BIRTH TO LIVING ROOM

Not long after the MDA meeting, I felt God's gentle but firm hand pushing me to make a faith-based approach to mental health care happen. He led me to start a group for individuals who, like me, needed God as part of their wellness plan.

For too long, people with mental illness had been misunderstood by the Church, denied the kind of support that would be helpful. Individuals with mental disorders were often blamed, told that their suffering was their own fault. Told that they had allowed themselves to wander too far from God.

Those who lived with mental health issues were missing the kind of spiritual care they needed—care that would help them accept their disability as a natural part of their make-up, care that would help them seek comfort and encouragement from their faith. They needed a message of assurance that God would walk with them through their highs and lows. They needed others like themselves to join them on that journey. They needed to know that they weren't alone.

I made an appointment with Pastor Don.

Having been introduced to the needs of people with mental health needs by me and the pastors' mental health workshop, he was open to hearing about how I felt God leading me to form a faith-based support group. Before long he gave me the green light to start planning.

My disorder had made a regular job impossible for me. I had never dreamed of doing anything like forming such a group. I had never heard of faith-based support groups addressing mental health problems. This was a brand-new thing I was undertaking. Where do I start?

I became a pioneer, travelling unknown territory with God my only guide.

There were times I doubted myself. "Who am I anyway doing something this big?"

From 1993 I'd been fighting the stigma of mental illness, first addressing a Christian audience in the year 2000. Now I would be giving direct help to those with such illnesses. I would be giving spiritual care to people who had for too long been ignored by the Church. My work was expanding. No longer was I only speaking *about* them, I was working *for* them.

But it was a huge task for a person who herself was living with mental illness. Anxiety was no stranger as I prepared. How I needed God!

Although most communication with my pastor took place by email, I'll never forget one meeting we had. I told him about how the story of David and Goliath often came to mind. I saw myself as the young David fighting a giant of a man. Goliath symbolized stigma for me. Stigma so huge that I couldn't see the head or feet. Only a massive body. Where should I aim my attack? Where do I start? How could I possibly be strong enough or clever enough?

David's response when King Saul doubted his ability to fight Goliath inspired me. His trust in God inspired me.

> *"Your servant has killed both the lion and the bear; this uncircumcised Philistine will be like one of them, because he has defied the armies of the living God. The Lord who rescued me from the paw of the lion and the paw of the bear will rescue me from the hand of this Philistine."* (1 Samuel 17:36-37)

I told my pastor how clear it had become to me that this big work I was taking on was God's, not mine at all. I shared how I marvelled at the difference that line of thinking was making to my resolve. God was giving me courage. I was able to trust him to stay with me and, in turn, I knew that I would try to stay with him.

I will always remember that holy time witnessing to my pastor. This wise man had been feeding me spiritually like I'd never been fed before. I trusted him. Much like a child with her father, I openly told him all I had in my heart. I shared how I felt God preparing me to do this big thing.

GOOD FRIDAY READING

As Good Friday approached in 2006, the pastor invited me to read two pieces from *A Firm Place to Stand*, the book I was in the middle of writing.

From *Wishing for an End*, I read:

> I am not often suicidal. My nature is to be positive, to try to see the best in everything. Yet that doesn't protect me from depression or even the occasional wish to die.
>
> Some time ago I again found myself in the depths, even making plans for a way out of life. I did not think of heaven or hell. All I could think of was how I wanted to stop the suffering that seemed always destined to return. I could not remember how it felt to be happy. Nor could I imagine ever feeling happy again.
>
> But I asked myself, what if Jesus had succumbed so quickly to the pain he faced? What if he had decided not to go to the cross? Where would we be?

Because of who he was, he could not have refused the cross. In Philippians 2:8, Paul wrote that *"though Jesus was human, he humbled himself and became obedient to death —even death on a cross."* He did not *want* to suffer the pain. But he knew his sacrifice would mean we would live. It was humanly possible for him to refuse the cross, but he didn't. His love for us was far too great.

I needed to look to Jesus as an example of how I should live. I can't be Jesus, but I can try to obey. If I can hold on to my desire to be like him, this will be possible. I need to stay close to God.

From *My Ultimate Source of Support*:

. . . God has said *"Never will I leave you; never will I forsake you."* (Hebrews 13:5).

My worst moments are occasional feelings of abandonment with its sense of doom, a chilly emptiness. There is nothing to hold onto. No hugs are tight enough to take away my sense of disconnectedness. I'm filled with a huge sense of insecurity. I cannot sleep.

All I know is that at times such as these, I need to go to my Bible. I need to pray. I need Jesus.

Some of the worst sufferings Jesus endured was the sense of abandonment he felt in the garden of Gethsemane as he tried to come to terms with the cross he knew he had to face. While he was in emotional anguish, his closest friends slept.

I can't fathom how horrifying it must have been to deal with abandonment in the face of having wrists and feet nailed to a cross and being left to die a slow, excruciating death. I'm sure the cross would not have been as painful had he known there were friends below expressing love and concern. But his friends deserted him.

When I'm in pain, I have Christ I can go to. Jesus did not have a Christ to turn to. He had to deal with the agony of the cross on his own, without friends and—for a time—even without God. He bore the weight entirely alone.

His great love for us made Jesus willing to walk to the cross. Love allowed him to endure the torture. Even as he hung there, wracked by physical pain, loneliness, and humiliation he begged his heavenly Father to forgive us. *"Father, forgive them, for they do not know what they're doing."* (Luke 23:34)

When I need to talk to someone and no one is home, or when phone lines are busy, Jesus is always there, waiting for me. When I feel I've been deserted, I search my Bible and pray, and Jesus hears my cries. I can pour out my heart to him and he fully understands. I cover myself warmly, laying my head on the pillow, and sleep peacefully once more. I know I'm taken care of. Thank you, Jesus.

After that reading, three people came to tell me their story of pain. They could relate to me. And they found comfort in knowing that I was a "safe" person to talk to. So good what happens when you share your personal emotional battles. It gives others permission to share their own battles as well.

And that's the beauty of our Living Room groups. That's what we do at Living Room.

I was amazed at how good it felt to have those three people be so honest with me. What a privilege it is to have someone share in that way with you! As I wrote in my book, I felt a lot like

Patch Adams did in the movie when he found out he could connect so well with the people in the mental hospital where he himself was a patient. "I connected to another human being!"

Like Patch Adams, I found out that I too really wanted to listen to people and learn about them. I wanted to help them with their troubles. And I wanted to do more of that. I wanted people with mental disorders to have the freedom to talk about their problems in a Christian setting—safely. This is how the idea for Living Room germinated.

Sharing my thoughts and feelings at such an appropriate time was a privilege. I was surprised to receive a good response from the congregation. Several individuals came to me in the weeks afterward to share the pain they had experienced in their own lives.

I found out that I was able to connect well with people who are in trouble. I learned that if I want to help people, I need to let them know that I understand them. I need to listen with compassion and love. I don't have to have answers. How freeing it is to know that's all I have to do to make a difference in people's lives!

In his devotional book, *Unto the Hills*, Billy Graham quotes a person saying. "To have suffered much is like knowing many languages. It gives the sufferer access to many more people." I sensed that happening in my own life. I feel as if I know many languages. I can relate to a wide variety of people.

I believe that this reading and the response it received did much to encourage me to start Living Room. I wanted to make a place where people could share their troubles and learn about Jesus and his love for them.

I SURRENDER ALL

My journalling, which I started in May 2006, consisted mostly of prayers. I wrote to God at all hours of the day, telling him of my passion, my hopes, and my dedication to serve.

During the spring and summer of 2006, while preparing to begin Living Room, I was greatly impacted by my reading of *Experiencing God: Knowing and Doing the Will of God,* a book by Henry Blackaby. A line that greatly encouraged me was this: "If you feel weak, limited, ordinary, you are the best material through which God can work!"

And I took to heart what Blackaby had to say about serving. I prayed,

> *"God, I want to be your servant. I know that I can do nothing on my own. I know that I cannot achieve the success you call me to achieve. I depend entirely on you to do your work through me. I know that you can do anything you choose to do. I give myself completely to you. Work through me any way you want to work. Show me where you are at work and include me in that work. I will not question your call. I will do any work you show me to do wherever that work is. Lord, accept the worship and dedication of your servant today."*

A few days after our first Living Room meeting on September 15th, I would write:

> In my openness in talking about my mental health problems and the evils of stigma, I guess I'm in a very real way sacrificing my own life—giving it away for a cause. The cause is more important than saving my own reputation, though I don't think I'm actually hurting it.

It feels good to have that courage. God has given me that courage. I wouldn't have it if he were not in my life. In fact, I think that God is speaking through me. As I mature, I'm finding it easier to say the things he would want me to say. Most of what I say, and the way I share, does not feel like it comes from me at all.

Each morning, I have to ask God to fill me up with him. I need to let him do his work. His heart; my hands. With God surrounding me and in me I can do all that he wants me to do.

"From everyone who has been given much, much will be demanded; and from the one who has been entrusted with much, much more will be asked." (Luke 12:48b)

On September 23rd I heard from Peter Andres who works with MCC Supportive Care Services (Communitas). He told me he had written a piece for BC Christian News, starting it with a paragraph of things I said in my book. Someone from the paper wants to talk to me about it. I prayed,

"This is what's so overwhelming, Lord. People are listening and valuing what I'm saying. Yet I feel so little, someone small who has been given a big job to do. But you are great, Lord, and you are inside me. I pray that I will remember always that it's all you who is doing the work. I'm only your hands. Help me to rest in that knowledge—the knowledge that it's not me alone who is being asked to do things or to be listened to. Thank you Lord, for allowing me to be your servant. Thank you for giving me so much to live for. Thank you for your love."

"I press on to take hold of that for which Christ Jesus took hold of me." (Philippians 3:12)

Some years later, on March 5, 2009, my resolve was strengthened, as it so often was:

Canadianchristianity.com has had a link to an article of mine on their home page for a long time now. The other day I saw that there were some new comments there. One was from a pastor whose wife has bipolar disorder. They have had to move from church to church finding acceptance nowhere. His wife has even been called a witch. His pain is obviously intense. He wants to find a support group for spouses. In this comment he is crying out to God, and I believe God hears his cries.

I believe that what I'm doing is very much joining God in his work. He is at work on this injustice and as long as I keep hearing stories like this pastor's, I will never give up this work. In fact, every time I hear something like this, my resolve is strengthened. Each time, my passion is aroused again.

MY CHURCH BECOMES SUPPORTIVE

At BPAC I was given several opportunities to speak to the congregation about mental illness. My struggles became common knowledge. Yet I had lots of dear friends to hug every Sunday morning. I loved them and felt loved in return. They all supported the church's new Living Room ministry. They asked about it. Prayed about it.

People who were known to have emotional problems, were frequently introduced to me because I was believed to know how to give support. I'm not sure how I felt about that. I liked supporting people, but wished some of the healthier people would not be afraid to do the supporting as well.

The wonderful thing is this: When Living Room became a part of our church ministry, people were less worried about being open about their mental health struggles. Living Room was often talked about. I don't think people felt too much shame being connected with it. I didn't, so they didn't either.

During a time of depression when I really didn't want to go on living, a good friend from church came to see me. She told me what a loss my life would be. Fixing her eyes on mine, she said, "No matter what you do or what you say, I'll always love you." She told me that she had prayed that God would let her be his hands for him as she had driven to my place. And he did.

It was through this godly woman that I fully came to understand how deep God's love is for me. Although I had become a Christian many years earlier, I had not fully grasped that until my friend showed me. Helen, also my Bible study leader, became my mentor.

She and another friend kept close tab on me, especially when my moods were not stable. They made it their business to learn what being bipolar means to me. And I gradually educated them, answering their many questions. They have seen me in many different states, and they kept loving me, unconditionally. They mothered me, and they let me mother them as well when they needed it. They encouraged me in all I did.

My pastor was also a great, compassionate support to me. I sent countless long emails to him (far too many)—when I was high and low. He went to the mental health seminar for pastors, especially to learn how to help me better. He was very excited about Living Room. He was my shepherd in this work. He represented God's tangible presence for me when I had problems dealing with the work I'd taken on.

If it weren't for such people in my life, I don't know if I would have written the book, *A Firm Place to Stand*. I know I would probably not have been able to start Living Room. Having a caring church congregation in place is important to how we who live with mental illness survive . . . and thrive!

DEVELOPING THE LIVING ROOM MODEL

When I began writing *A Firm Place to Stand*, I had not thought of creating Living Room. Living room was born out of reflection and the writing process. God was working in me as I poured out my thoughts and as I was mentored, pastored, and prayed for. The group became the heart of all I did.

I had experienced the secular mood disorder support groups of MDA. Their peer-based support meetings were an example we followed, but with a strong spiritual focus.

Excerpted from *A Firm Place to Stand*:

> Living Room is not a therapy group. It's not led by professionals. Instead, it is based on self-help, facilitated by people who themselves have a mood disorder. By helping each other, we help ourselves.
>
> An important rule at living Room is "no advising, no fixing, no saving, no setting each other straight," borrowed from Parker J Palmer's ground rules for his Quaker "Circle of Trust." No one has all the answers. And we don't want to make the same mistakes Job's friends made when they tried to support him in his grave illness and losses. They tried to fix Job by advising him to repent of his sin, wrongly assuming that was the problem.
>
> How can the Church support people with mental illness? Not by advising, trying to fix, trying to save. We need to

help people carry their burden of pain. That means that we should be there for them when they need to talk about what they're going through, trying to understand, trying to sympathize, to feel with them. In this way, we show acceptance and love. When we advise, it's as though we're being judgmental. We should demonstrate the unconditional love God taught us, through Jesus Christ, to have.

Everyone at Living Room groups is fully accepted, no matter where they are emotionally or spiritually. We share openly, knowing that this is a safe place where honesty is valued and no one judges. We support each other with compassion because we all travel similar journeys.

At Living Room, we talk about our faith and receive prayer. We study Scripture to learn how to cope with our mental health challenges. By sharing our troubles with people who understand, we find healing. At Living Room, we can shed feelings of guilt and shame because we no longer have to keep our mental health problems a secret.

From the beginning, I felt that Christians everywhere needed faith-based support like this. I understood what a group like this could do for Christians with mood disorders, and I saw it as a pilot project that could serve as a model for other groups. To encourage others to form Living Room groups, I wrote a set of manuals describing how to set up and facilitate a group. This project was followed by a website, put together by my son Cornelius and his wife Jeanette.

The founding Living room group at BPAC brought me great joy. As I wrote *Riding the roller Coaster* and *A Firm Place to Stand*, I could only imagine the people I was writing for— people who, like me, suffered from mood disorders. Through my group, I came to see and talk to those people, eat with them, and walk with them. I showed them what God had taught me about living a tough life and helped them realize how much God loves us.

I felt the Holy Spirit at work in me as I welcomed members to the meetings. Showing them that God's love did not require effort. God was present in this work. I was doing what he created me to do, and that made me strong. After meetings, I prayed joyously. *"Thank you, God, thank you."*

THE FIRST GROUPS WERE BORN

We called the group "Living Room," a name coined by Dr. John Toews, a proponent of better church support who inspired its organization.

The founding of Living Room became an outreach project in partnership with MDA, who trained us how to facilitate. We advertised in their newsletter as well as the local community newspapers. We were surprised at how well the small announcements in the papers were noticed. The calls trickled in at a steady pace. "What do you mean by faith-based mental health support?" I think some thought it was too good to be true.

One person who did not appear to be a believer asked me to describe how we did things. He said that the way I talked about how important faith is to me didn't turn him off. He'd like to come and explore it.

The people who came to Living Room were hurting, not only from the symptoms of their mental illness, but more so from the way they had been treated. Here they were welcomed to a spiritual home that accepted them, despite their mental health difficulties. Their faith and mental health were addressed together. Living Room became their church.

Living Room and the light it gradually brought to Christian understanding was much needed. The message of Jesus Christ and his care for the outcast brought comfort and emotional strength to individuals who had been hungry for spiritual care.

The founding group, facilitated by me and cofacilitated by Janice K, met at BPAC two afternoons a month with lunch provided. A second group started a month later, meeting two evenings a month at New Life Community Church in Burnaby. This group was facilitated by Mark J and cofacilitated by Graham H.

At BPAC, we met in a large, cavernous hall in the basement. It was not the coziest meeting place, but what helped was putting a table in the centre of the hall, covered with a colorful tablecloth. A centerpiece was in the middle and for a few years there were dishes of chocolates. Boxes of Kleenex completed the setting.

As the group grew, the table grew. We put several long tables together until it became huge, enough for the 20 who were often in attendance. Gathering around one single table was a must for me. It spelled togetherness. It made it easy to talk with each other over lunch and coffee.

My group drew people from the community and beyond. They came from far and wide. Members came as they felt the need, so we never knew how many would come. It was always a surprise. Almost always one or two new people came. Many came by word of mouth. The day before the meeting, we called to encourage everybody to come. It helped them feel connected.

The introductions were conducted much like AA's. Going around the table, each person gave their first name, and if they wished, what their diagnosis is. Doing so helped them feel there's nothing to be ashamed of. After prayer, we went into a devotional time. It was an interactive devotional where the facilitator introduced a theme and everyone was given a chance to have input.

Before going into small groups, we prayed, asking God to fill us with his love and to help us share that love with each other. I believe that prayer had an impact on the way the sharing time went. There was much love in the group.

Living Room is important to the people who come. Some of them have been hurt by misunderstanding friends. All of us at Living Room, including the leaders, understand what it's like to live with mood disorders and so we know how to support each other. By sharing our stories, we find out we're not alone.

CHAPTER FIVE

RAISING MENTAL HEALTH AWARENESS
2006

A FIRM PLACE TO STAND

While I was developing plans for the Living Room ministry, I was hard at work writing my book, *A Firm Place to Stand: Finding Meaning in a Life with Bipolar Disorder.* I hoped that this would contribute to raising mental health awareness in the Church. With this autobiographical account I tried to demonstrate that even a person with a major mental health disorder could be a strong Christian. I showed how God was able to turn my weakness into strength, transforming me into a leader, an activist, and the founder of Living Room.

The book dispelled the stigma of mental illness and encouraged Christians to lovingly welcome sufferers into congregations by understanding them and supporting them in practical ways. It showed that it is possible to have a mental disorder yet be close to God and derive strong support from a growing relationship with Christ.

I believe this must have been the most difficult book I've written. There was so much to discuss and I wanted to do a thorough job of it. Work on the book became an ongoing struggle as I was constantly distracted by the need to write articles and emails as I reached out in numerous ways to have God's message heard. So much to cover!

The story I tell is how a very sick young person grew to have faith in God and was gradually transformed into someone who was—for the most part—joyful and grateful to be alive. It is truly amazing where God has taken me since those early years when I spent nine months in a mental hospital. For twenty-five years I was thought to be schizophrenic and received only anti-psychotic drugs—no mood stabilizers. My struggles were later shown to be caused by bipolar disorder.

I tried hard to find a publisher, but in the end had to self-publish in 2008 using Word Alive Press.

Learning to promote my book was not straightforward. In August 2007 I was overwhelmed by all that needed to be done. I knew that I was in a position to do some good, but how could I best do it?

> *"Please, God, lead me in the best way to go. I know I'm not on my own with this. This is, after all, your work and not my own. I shouldn't worry so much. I should realize that the burden is not all mine to carry. Help me take aim with my writing tools and publicity in a way that will do the most good."*

In the library I found some books on how to do such promotion. I made a list of the things I needed to prepare to send out to the press. Then I sat down and wrote the most difficult part of it, a press release.

At the time, there was a series in the *Vancouver Sun* about the stigma towards mental illness. I was able to pick up on that and include material in my promotional material to talk about the stigma that some Christians still harbor. I tried to focus on the need for the unconditional love that Christ modelled for us. I tried to show how tragic it was that the Church is not following his example. I wrote about the damage caused to people who believe in God but are driven from the Church because they feel judged there. *A Firm Place to Stand* could prompt discussion on a lot of important issues.

OUR NEED IS GREAT

I have lived with bipolar disorder as a person who didn't believe in God. And I've lived with bipolar as someone who learned to have faith in Jesus Christ. And though my faith did not "heal" me, it brought healing and I have become a stronger person because of it.

Trusting in God has removed a lot of the fear I had. I don't become anxious as often. I know that I'm on a spiritual journey that will never end until I go to heaven. Some anxiety and some fear will always be part of my life but I live with a hope that keeps me well more than I would otherwise be. And although I know that depression will still periodically come, I've learned that I'm a different person in some way every time I come back into the light. My moods teach me things, even if it's only to have better compassion for others who suffer in some way.

The Bible says,

> ". . . we rejoice in our sufferings, because we know that suffering produces perseverance; perseverance, character; and character, hope. And hope does not disappoint us, because God has poured out his love into our hearts by the Holy Spirit, who he has given us." (Romans 5:3-5)

Although suffering is painful the pain does build character.

I think the greatest thing I've learned since I began following Christ, was that God loves me unconditionally, no matter what. When I periodically go through feelings of abandonment and darkness, I try to remember Jesus who is well acquainted with those feelings. He also suffered greatly. God knows what our pain is like. When we suffer, he suffers with us. We are not alone. I can cling to that knowledge.

I have known of God's love for a long time, but I haven't always felt it or grasped just how great it truly is. Yet when I did, I became more confident, more assured of my worth. And all I knew that I wanted to do, was to work for him, to help others understand how wide and long and high and deep his love is.

In August 2006 I was asked to facilitate a session of a secular support group for the MDA. The meeting was a heavy one. I did a good job facilitating. It felt natural to me. I only had to listen, respond, wait for others to respond, and then move on to the next person when I thought we'd spent enough time with someone.

But when I got home from that meeting, I just had to get on my knees and pray for some of the people I met. There was such a lot of deep pain and so many have nowhere to turn. Proper care is difficult to get. And some of the people simply didn't have the money for a reasonable place to live.

One big thing missing from the meeting was the hope of Jesus Christ. If that could have been talked about, those people would have more to hang on to. Thank God, we will have the opportunity to share that in the Living groups we'll be forming.

Albert Schweitzer talked about how those who have good fortune in some areas of their life should share it with others. I have so much good fortune and feel called to share myself with others.

The pain and suffering is so huge, yet we in our cozy lives tend to be insulated from seeing it. It's when you get close to people with such problems that you become more fully aware of the tragedies in the world. I feel like some of my protection has been rubbed off and I am in touch with some of the pain people are going through.

THE FIRST MEETING

Friday, September 15, 2006, was the big day—the day of the first meeting of the founding Living Room group.

For a few weeks, I had felt nervous about facilitating. The day before, I prayed:

> *"Lord, I feel I'm doing what you called me to do. This makes me feel strong and focused. Help me to stay close to you, to walk in your power. Thank you for showing me a way to serve you that makes my life meaningful. It brings me joy.*

> *"Please help me keep this well feeling that I have right now. Yet I know I have a disorder that can change this wellness for no apparent reason. I'm walking a tightrope as I try to maintain balance and stability.*

> *'For we are God's handiwork, created in Christ Jesus to do good works, which God prepared in advance for us to do.'* (Ephesians 2:10)

> *"Yes, I feel that you have made me for this. My whole life has led me in this direction. Thank you, God, for making me the way you did."*

The next day I was eager to begin. Even before I started, I felt at home in the facilitating role and sensed that this was work God genuinely wanted me to do.

A tiny group gathered around a small table on that first day. My co-facilitator and me and a couple of others.

Fifteen minutes into the meeting, almost having given up on anyone else coming, we heard the heavy footsteps of a man clomping down the long staircase. When he appeared, I was a bit taken aback. He looked somewhat disheveled and, to be honest, he scared me a bit.

After introductions, we started discussing the day's topic, "fear." After a long interval with no one speaking, the man was the first person to speak, surprising us with his gruff voice. "I have fear." This began our first sharing time.

This person, whom I'll call Terry, was a person I cared a lot about. He was a regular with us for many years, sharing his fears, but also sharing his love for God.

The pastor sat in on the first half of the meeting. I was grateful for him and his support.

I had received an email from him the night before saying, "We are entering new waters with this ministry." He really didn't know where God would take us, but he was excited about it. I didn't know where God was leading either but knew we should take this a step at a time. We need to follow him, joining him in the work he is doing in the world rather than expecting him to join us. I need to walk with him, my hand securely holding onto his.

A Living Room group is an example of how the Church can provide tangible support for people with depression, anxiety, and bipolar disorder. Later on, people with all kinds of mental health issues were to find a welcome there. In the back of my mind, I wondered. Is this the germ of something bigger? Might this spread to other churches?

SERMON PROPOSAL TO PASTORS

From the time I started planning Living Room, I kept a journal, using it to write letters to God at all hours of the day. I usually wrote first thing in the morning during my quiet time. But I kept the notebook with me all day, stopping to write whenever I had thoughts I wanted to share with God. God was never far away. Always with me, ready to hear what I was writing to him.

As I've been going through the writings I did in 2006 when I was starting my Living Room ministry, I can see that my mood was elevated during much of that time. My days were full of activities. Ministry work, housework, getting my message out to all who would hear. Far too busy. Feeling guilty at those times when I wasn't engaged in something to further the cause.

In an effort to find the peace that eluded me, I started many of my morning journal entries with words from Psalm 23:1-3: *"The Lord is my shepherd, I shall not want. He makes me lie down in green pastures, he leads me beside quiet waters, he refreshes my soul."*

On November 25, I prayed,

> *"Lord, please help me feel comfort, peace and rest, without a sense of guilt."*

And yet, the very next day I decided to send out a sermon proposal for pastors to just about everyone I knew.

The sermon proposal I sent went like this:

Dear Friends,

A friend of mine, someone with bipolar disorder, recently said to me,

"I've gone to church nearly all my life and I've just heard about mental illnesses mentioned once, and just in passing. When I was hospitalized, some people came from the church, but they just prayed for the devil to leave me."

As someone who also lives with bipolar disorder, I find this tragic. For a person who is already suffering to be told she's not right with God is painful. It damages a person's relationship with her Christian friends and her church. Some of those who are suffering, even come to believe that it *is* the devil that is the cause of their troubles and refuse to take the medication that would help them survive.

Would a person in hospital because of a heart attack, a stroke, or Alzheimer's be prayed for in this way? Can you imagine how that would make them feel?

I believe churches should, at least once a year, receive a message from the pulpit on the truths about mental illness. I know that pastors don't usually preach about illnesses, but in this case, congregants need to learn how to separate the spiritual from the medical. Too many are uninformed and make things worse because they don't know how to best support people who are going through emotional trauma. The kind of support such individuals need is very similar to the support people with physical illness need: practical help with things like meals and transportation, and a sympathetic ear. Church leaders can help their church family learn how to provide this.

There are two excellent opportunities each year for such a

sermon. This upcoming year, May 7-13 is Mental Health Week. In October there is a Mental Health Awareness Week as well.

If you know someone who is a pastor, could you please forward this message on to him or her? You would be doing a big service for the many who suffer from mental illness and need to be understood.

Many thanks,
Marja Bergen
Author of *Riding the Roller Coaster: Living With Mood Disorders*

The next day, it was as though I was caught up in a current when all the responses started coming in:

An email from Wood Lake Books, publisher of *Riding the Roller Coaster*. Communitas wants to use this as a topic for its annual letter to pastors; MDA is suggesting I write something for their newsletter, which they would then send to churches; Faith Net, a part of the National Association for Mental Illness (NAMI), asked permission to re-publish my post on their website.

My one letter was being passed on to numerous people. A supporter later reported that it had ended up on nineteen different sites on the web.

I felt like a David in writing that sermon proposal. God was with me. My aim was accurate. I felt strong. I could clearly see the giant I was facing. I had to address pastors. People need to understand how to help people with mental health issues. And who is better equipped to tell them? Who do they most respect? Their pastors.

Can a sheep rest beside such a rushing current?

I SPEAK TO A SECULAR AUDIENCE

MDA invited me to represent them in a panel discussion on *Depression in the Elderly* which took place on October 5, 2006 at Douglas College in New Westminster. There were three on the panel, Dr. Jeremy Sable, a geriatric psychiatrist, Dr. Art Hister, a family physician and columnist, and me, a person living with mental health challenges. I felt honored to be part of this, and when first invited to speak, was quite overwhelmed.

But I spoke better than I had thought I would, even though I did go off track a number of times. I thanked God for helping me speak from the heart in a powerful way. In the past I would never have thought I could do that. God was definitely with me.

Afterwards, quite a few people, including the two doctors, told me that they had appreciated what I said. A social worker from Richmond Mental Health was quite excited about what I'm doing with the support groups. He told me that my timing for this was perfect. We exchanged email addresses and phone numbers, wanting to make sure to stay in touch.

A couple of weeks later, what I had said appeared in the Fraser Health newsletter.

A friend sent me Revelations 3:7-8, saying she thought it applied to me:

> *"What he opens no one can shut, and what he shuts no one can open. I know your deeds. See, I have placed before you an open door that no one can shut. I know that you have little strength, yet you have kept my word and have not denied my name."*

And I prayed,

> *"Lord, I guess I have more than a foot in the door. You have opened it wide for me. Let me be worthy. Let me always remember that I'm your servant. You are with me. Thank you for the courage you've given me. Help me, Lord, to make the ripples that I've been starting into waves. And Lord, please help me stay well."*

ABSENT MINDED

On October 26, 2006, I wrote the following to my blogging pals:

I've been so stable lately, so cool, calm, and collected. But today, I feel like I could cry.

You may remember I had two accidents recently, all within a month. In the last one, my car was almost totalled. Today I was close to getting into another accident, and it was my fault. Ever since my last accident, my driving has felt sloppy. I have trouble focusing. I don't know if I should be driving any more. I could kill someone or be killed.

And I'm thinking about how my life would change if I were without a car. It's depressing to consider that. I know I have a husband who drives, but our lives are so separate from each other. He would not want to drive me around to all the things I do. I can't imagine a life without the independence my car gives me.

Tomorrow is a meeting of our Living Room group. I was so looking forward to it. Still am. There are quite a few people who have called and I'm eager to meet them and to lead a good meeting. I need to pray. I need to strengthen up and put these worries aside. At least for a while.

Next week I will visit my family doctor and describe what has been happening to my thinking lately. The narrowness of my focus, losing track of time because I can only concentrate on one thing at a time. Is this a sign of a mind growing old? But I'm only 60!! My husband says that I've just been preoccupied lately. But that's no excuse.

Please pray for Living Room tomorrow. Pray that I will get over the shock of this near-accident and place my attention on what I so love to do—to support people with mood disorders and to help them grasp how great God's love for them is.

POSTSCRIPT:

As I write this in 2024, at age 78, I still have the same problem. Absent-mindedness. Caused by being too focussed on my work perhaps? I stopped driving around 2014 because I couldn't pay attention. My mind is so often elsewhere. I have to be careful crossing the street. I've been known to run into people with my walker.

CHAPTER SIX

LIVING ROOM
2007

LIVING ROOM – MY HOME
My Prayer:

Lord, I've been doing a lot of thinking about why I feel better at Living Room than I do anywhere else. I feel completely myself there, not worrying about what people will think of me. That's not how I've been in the past. In fact, when I was younger I had social anxiety disorder. I wasn't comfortable at all in group situations. Afraid to talk to people I didn't know well. Today I still feel somewhat that way in social situations.

But at Living Room I'm an outgoing hostess. I love welcoming people as they come in. All of them are dealing with some kind of mental health condition. I want to make them feel at home, fully accepted. The greeting is not anything I have to work at. It just happens.

Why is it so easy to be myself at Living Room? Why does the welcoming come so easily and naturally?

Is it because of what I started praying shortly after I started following you Lord? Many times, I asked you to fill me with your love and to help me share that love with the people I meet. I recall the warm glow I felt inside as you filled me up. Was it that prayer that started it all?

Whenever I prayed like this in the morning, you always answered. As I went through the day I was able to share your love with others without effort. It wasn't anything I did. I know it was your doing, God. It was you working through me. Thank you so much for this. It has made such a difference in my life.

Lord, these days I don't consciously offer up that prayer anymore, but it seems like I don't need to. You know that I long to share your love, especially with those who suffer in the way I myself do. I know what people who come to Living Room need. So many are feeling the effects of stigma. They are hungry for acceptance and understanding. They need what I need. Open arms. The kind of love you showed to the sick and the outcast.

You know God, although I can speak reasonably well about the things I have a passion for, I'm not always a fluent speaker, often unable to recall the simplest words. It seems to be getting worse the older I get . . . or is it all the meds I'm taking? Yet at Living Room, though I spend about 45 minutes speaking and leading an interactive devotional time, I feel completely at ease. Although I stumble, fishing for words, I get the message across, just being myself.

But stumbling on my words is not such a bad thing at Living Room. When the group hears me doing so without embarrassment they easily join in the conversation, knowing they don't have to worry about such things. When I come across authentically, everyone is encouraged to be authentic. They, like me, can relax at Living Room, sharing openly and honestly.

HOLY JOY

From the beginning of Living Room, I found that when I shared God's love with others, I loved myself more. By sharing God's love through Living Room meetings, through my blogging, and through giving one on one support, I experienced what I've come to look on as a "holy joy" — something priceless that can't be obtained in any other way.

"Carry each other's burdens," the Bible says, *"and in this way you will fulfill the law of Christ."* (Gal 6:2) And God helps us carry our burdens, as brothers and sisters.

The Holy Spirit must have been with me because I remember well those hours after Living Room meetings when I went home to the quiet of my bedroom, savoring this holy joy.

I prayed, *"Thank you, God, for your presence in the midst of our troubles. Having you close fills me with a quiet joy."*

Years later, after a meeting in May 2012, I would pray:

"Where does this deep, deep gratitude after Living Room come from, Lord, after being at a gathering of 26 people, all experiencing emotional problems? It's a mystery to me how the intensity of this feeling comes about. I don't look for it. It just happens . . . like your Spirit. Mysterious. Inexplicable, but Real.

"All I can do is to say, "Thank you, thank you, thank you!" I'm so grateful that you've made me part of this work you're doing. There have been times when I've done something very uncommon for me. I've actually gotten down on my knees.

"Is it the leading of the devotional that brings this about? Is it the sharing of who you are to me? Is it how members of the group share their innermost feelings and thoughts in the breakout groups?

"Whatever this mystery is, you're blessing me hugely through this work. Thank you for that. And I pray that in some mysterious way, the people who come will also receive your blessing."

MY PICTURE ON THE FRONT PAGE

On February 15, 2007, I got a call from Rennie Hoffman, the Executive Director of MDA, asking if I would do an interview with the Vancouver Sun. Within an hour a columnist called.

He told me that the paper was doing a three-part series on depression. He asked what I feel like when I'm depressed. I told him a few of the feelings I get, like not being able to see the brilliance of a colorful garden. But then I also told him a few things he wasn't asking about, like the highs I experience with my bipolar condition and what they do to me. I told him how the higher my mood goes, the deeper I drop.

Five days later a photographer came to take my picture. To my surprise, he wanted more than a head and shoulder shot. He took me to the rollercoaster at an amusement park a few miles away and photographed me at the base of it. He took dozens of shots with me holding my *Riding the Roller Coaster* book. That book had been out for almost eight years, and now it was getting fresh attention.

Later I called Wood Lake Books, my publisher, and let him know. He was excited as well and got the marketing department to try and get copies onto store shelves again.

That evening, I tried my best to come down off the mountaintop by listening to music and ironing. We ended up with a lot more clothes to wear.

On the morning of Saturday, February 24, I was amazed when I opened the Sun and saw my picture on the front page under the prominent headline, "Defeating Depression." It took up much of the page. Inside were two full pages with information about depression . . . and another, rather unflattering photo of me. I guess it was a good description of what a depressed person might look like.

What I said in the interview was part of a big article, interspersed with quotes from other people. It was very informative. A huge stigma buster. As you can well imagine, I was excited and happy. I quietly hoped that this would get my book into a lot more people's hands.

MENTAL HEALTH SERVICE AT CHURCH

In honor of Mental Health Week, BPAC had a special mental health service on May 6, 2007. In his sermon, *Out of the Shadows,* Pastor Don talked about the importance of being a caring community for those dealing with mental health problems. He spoke of how we need to look at Jesus in how we live and how we treat others. There was a wonderful touch of humor here and there. All in all, an uplifting service.

Three speakers from our Living Room group spoke openly and from the heart. And the congregation was warm and welcoming. They received a hearty applause. Many stayed behind to talk with them.

I feel that the best part of the service was the performance of the song, *Redeemed,* composed by one of our Living Room members. She played the piano while her friend sang.

At the end of the service, the pastor mentioned how Living Room isn't complete without chocolate. And it's true, at that time, we had dishes of chocolate on the table at all our meetings. We considered it good "medicine." The pastors' wives served chocolates at the door as worshippers left the sanctuary.

The mental health service surpassed my expectations. It was so wonderful that I spent the rest of the day in a bit of a daze, trying to process it all and listening to the CD that was made.

This was a good example of how well a church could be supportive of people with mental health issues. Next to medication and faith in God, there's nothing else as important as having the support of your church family. When I struggled with depression I knew there were friends at church who would be there for me and pray for me. I knew they wouldn't be judgmental or think there was something spiritually wrong with me.

As a result of that service, a couple of people in the church indicated they would like to come to the next Living Room meeting. By making our mental health an okay thing to talk about, we who are suffering know that we don't need to be alone in our struggles.

Living Room met the next Friday and the meeting had a party atmosphere. We set up four tables joined together, making one huge table that would seat 18 people. My co-facilitator thought that I was perhaps overdoing it. But we ended up with 20 in attendance. We celebrated by bringing out a cake with sparklers on it.

Although I'm happy about the success of our group, I also felt overwhelmed. How long can we continue doing this before it becomes unwieldy? We usually like to have some discussion based on the devotional but had to forego that this day because of lack of time. With ten people in each breakout group, there wasn't much time for everyone to share.

I could see how more faith-based groups like this needed to be formed. The need was greater than my church could adequately respond to. A week later, I began writing a manual as a guide for churches who wished to do what we had done.

CREATING MANUALS

In May 2007, just over a week after the mental health service I sat down to start putting together the Creating Living Room manual. But it took some courage getting started. *"Help me, Lord, please, to get the juices flowing."*

That morning, I had been reading in Exodus about how Moses felt when God told him to free his people. He said, *"Who am I, that I should go to Pharaoh and bring the Israelites out of Egypt?"* (Ex 3:11)

That's just like what I had put in an email to a friend the night before. "Who do I think I am?"

But God told Moses that he would be with him. And I know that God will be with me too if I trust him. I believe that anything is possible through God. But I need to believe. I need to have hope.

> *"So, I ask you, Lord, to be with me, to work through me, as I begin to write this manual. Let my words be your words. I thank you for helping me find a life of significance. I thank you for giving me such an adventurous way to serve you."*

In the end I wrote two manuals: *Creating Living Room* and *Facilitating Living Room*. (How much better it would have been if I had combined the two into one document!)

The first manual was for church leaders and people with mood disorders who wanted to know how to set up a group. It gave a description of the Living Room concept. The second was a facilitator's guide, for which the MDA manual provided guidance.

When I was finished the Creating Living Room manual, I printed off one or two copies and put them in a report cover to see what it would look like. This was all I felt we could afford. But when I showed them to my psychiatrist, Dr. Long, a big supporter of this effort, his response was, "Is this all it's going to be? You need to have it printed properly." And he got his check book out and wrote a check to cover the cost of printing.

Dr. Long felt that what we were doing with Living Room was similar to how Alcoholics Anonymous got its start. He felt it had great promise.

Steve Thiessen, CEO of Communitas offered to send 100 - 150 copies of the Creating Living Room manuals to pastors, along with a covering letter from him. He would be paying for those copies. How wonderful!

We now had funding to complete the printing.

Soon after, I went through MDA's binder of materials and pulled out the most important items that were applicable to our group, including them in our Facilitating Living Room manual.

The next step—a most pressing need—was to create booklets of sample interactive devotionals for group use. I needed to help new groups that formed understand what they could do at their meetings and to assure that Christian principles would be taught and adhered to. Living Room participants needed to be confident of Christ's great love and how he could transform their lives.

The devotionals, along with the manuals, were eventually made available on the Living Room website as free downloadable pdf files. Living Room's work could go on, even if I weren't available to carry on in the way I was.

Today, in 2024, sixty of those interactive devotionals are still available online, as well as 230 devotionals for personal use. They can be downloaded from https://marjabergen.com/devotionals.

TOO MUCH FOR A SINGLE PERSON

On June 21, 2007, I talked to Peter Biggs from *BC Christian News*. He wants more material on faith and mental health. Much more. I think he would like me to be a regular contributor. Will this exposure help me find a publisher for *A Firm Place to Stand*?

In my journal this morning I made a list of all the things I'm trying to do and I'm overwhelmed. What I'm trying to do should be the work of an organization, not a single person!

How did I get into all this? Is this mountain the product of a bipolar mind? I haven't been hypomanic lately. Yet I'm always ambitious. I always have dreams. These things don't change. They're part of who I am.

But I can now see that I have built a very high tower, brick by brick, not realizing how high it might become or how I would manage it or how I could keep it from toppling.

The good thing is that if I can't do some of the things I've personally committed myself to no one will be hurt . . . too much. I can let things go. Yet it's hard not to take advantage of opportunities. Letting go of some of the ones that have come along lately would be a shame. So, I'm feeling pressured.

I am excited about having finished the Creating Living Room manual to help other Living Rooms get started. I know it will be a powerful tool, helping other churches see the value of such a group and showing them how to set one up. Forming a Living Room group gives churches an opportunity to respond to Christ's call to love and help people who are all too often shunned in the community. Having such a group in the church is a good way to help build understanding within its congregation. It will help make mental illness a more acceptable topic of conversation.

I've been hearing that people in other communities are now showing interest in starting up groups. I would like to be able to be there to support these new groups. I will also have to work at writing another manual for facilitators and another with sample interactive devotional material. With those projects and writing for the website my son and his wife are creating, I have much writing to do.

"God, please help me stay well. There's too much good work to do."

I shared with my pastor in an email:

My tower has been built by God, and if I trust in him I know it will not topple. Building such towers is a bipolar thing. It's the kind of thing that can push a person into mania. But if I keep the understanding that it's God at work, not me, I don't think mania will happen. This creativity I have is what makes me often say that I consider my bipolar disorder a gift from God. It can be painful to live with, yet it *is* a gift too.

For such a long time my main goal in life has been to reduce the stigma towards mentally ill people within the church. For so long I have been striving to educate

Christians by writing articles, promoting a pastor's mental health workshop, and writing a book. But now things are coming together.

In May, canadianchristianity.com published my testimony. Soon they will be publishing an article I wrote for CMHA (BC Div) a couple of years ago, *Mental Illness: The Result of Sin?*

And there's more. A woman in Abbotsford, a town 45 minutes from here, is working to start a Living Room group in her church. This could be the beginning of my dream to see Living Room groups in many churches.

Not long ago, a call came from a therapist wanting to learn about Living Room. He is hoping to send his Christian clients to us. So often they feel that they're bad Christians when they're depressed and they don't want to take medication. Living Room would be helpful because it draws from the Bible and recognizes the medical nature of mood disorders.

It's amazing where God leads us when we let him! It's time to make a list. Time to set priorities.

CHAPTER SEVEN

GIVING SUPPORT
2007

SUPPORTING FRIENDS WITH DEPRESSION

On June 13, 2007, I wrote to my blogging pals:

My next project is to write an article for canadian-christianity.com about how Christians can give support to friends suffering from depression. You may think, "Wouldn't the kind of support Christians give be the same as support given by anyone else?"

The answer is, yes of course. But the truth is that many still believe that depression has a spiritual basis. Also, there are spiritual ways of supporting people by praying with them or by letting them know you're praying. There's also the story of Job and his friends. Too many forget that story when they're trying to help depressed friends. The way in which Job's friends tried, but failed to help, has lessons for us.

My neighbor has been telling me about her depressed friend who she is trying to give support to. "I don't know what to tell her to do anymore," she said. "I don't know how to help her." But that tends to be the problem with many people who are trying to help. They think that giving advice is going to fix depression. The truth is that they only need to be available to listen with compassion. And patiently continue to love.

For most people that's a hard thing to do. Everyone wants to fix things for others when that is an impossible thing to do. Trying to do so could easily make a depressed person feel worse.

At the time I wrote the above, I was reading *A Hidden Wholeness*, a book by the Quaker writer, Parker J. Palmer. Palmer identified an approach called *Practices of the Circle of Trust* to facilitate some ground rules for groups to create a safe space to learn and grow together. This is the kind of group I hoped Living Room could be.

A line from this book made its way into Living Room's Facilitators' Manual: "No fixing, no saving, no advising, no setting each other straight."

This rule is one we should try to follow when we help individuals through their emotional problems. The important thing for us is to hear each other. When we try to fix each other's problems it's indirectly a way of escaping further involvement.

From *A Hidden Wholeness*:

> A circle of trust consists of relationships that are neither invasive nor evasive. In this space, we neither invade the mystery of another's true self nor evade another's struggles. We stay present to each other without wavering, while stifling any impulse to fix each other up.

DO I WANT TO GET WELL?

If you are like me, battling depression or other mood difficulties, you might be able to identify with my reflections below. If you are supporting a person with such problems, my experience will give you some insight into what we live with.

On May 22, 2007, I wrote:

I've almost finished reading a great book by Mark Buchanan called *The Rest of God: Restoring Your Soul by Restoring Sabbath*. Something he said hit me very hard and made me look at something I've never considered before. He said, "It's the most natural thing to befriend your sickness, even, after long association, to depend upon it." Buchanan carries on by talking about some of the people Jesus healed, "Their entire lives . . . have taken shape around their injuries or diseases."

In John 5:6 Jesus asks a crippled man, "*Do you want to get well?*" That seems to be an odd thing to ask a person and, to think that a person doesn't really want to get well, might make us think ill of them. We might think they are feeling sorry for themselves or wanting pity. But this man had been crippled all of his 38 years. No one had ever expected anything from him. He had never had responsibilities. To suddenly be well would mean a drastic new way of living, a way of living that would be hard to adjust to.

And this made me think that perhaps I'm a bit like that. To be perfectly honest, having lived with bipolar disorder for my entire forty years of adult life, my illness does, in large part, define me. A major part of my current life involves raising awareness about mental health issues and supporting others who live with mood disorders.

My bipolar disorder is responsible for the kind of person I've become. When my mood is elevated, which often happens, I become super creative. I value that in myself. My moods are what make me who I am . . . though I would love to get rid of those depressions.

If Jesus asked me, "*Do you want to get well?*" would I say yes? I'm sure that if he had offered to make me well when I was twenty or thirty, or forty, I would have gladly said yes. I would then have been able to go back to school perhaps and start a career. My illness has kept me from that, the stress being too great. I've tried. I might have been able to make photography a full-time career.

But now, at 61, I have learned to turn the bipolar into something good. Something that's perhaps better than a photography career. I've learned how to help others cope with their illness. I've learned to build awareness. That has become my life. I could not do these things without experiencing the disorder myself.

But although I still have bipolar disorder, I think Jesus *has* made me well. In helping others, I am helping myself. The work I do gives me great joy. Although my life is filled with trials, I love the life I live.

It is truly amazing how so many artists, musicians, and especially writers, have had bipolar disorder or depression. Personally, I thrive on creative projects. I'm a photographer, writer, cookbook author, knitter, cross stitch embroiderer, and publisher of inspirational booklets. I've initiated innovative projects.

As I matured, I learned to take on leadership roles. Living Room is my latest venture. It's something that excites me and gives me opportunities for creative planning.

Not sure, but perhaps all this has something to do with my disorder. It's partly because of this that I'm not unhappy about having bipolar disorder. The meds contain my moods so that they don't overwhelm me too much. I stay on the page.

Heightened sensitivity has influenced my spiritual life as well. When my mood is elevated, the words of the Bible speak powerfully to me, in a way that would not be possible if I were stable. Not that the way I read it is an "insane" response, but I absorb the meaning in a more intensive way than if my mood were flatter. Scripture becomes more understandable to me. The meaning I get out of it goes deeper.

I've accomplished much, things I would never have been inspired to do if it were not for my frequent highs. But it's been costly as well. All too often, these highs are followed by periods of depression.

And yet, when I look back, I can say I am grateful for all God has given me. Life has been difficult, but it has also been an exciting adventure . . . and it continues to be that.

MY TESTIMONY PUBLISHED

2007 was a busy year: developing the broader Living Room ministry, facilitating my group, helping individuals in crisis. I was also doing the big work of pioneering mental health awareness in the Church through much speaking and writing, which included writing the book, *A Firm Place to Stand.*

In early June, my testimony, *No Longer Alone*, went online at canadianchristianity.com. In August, it would appear as an almost full page of print in BC Christian News.

Towards the end of the testimony, I wrote:

> The urge to speak out and to support others with mental health challenges never leaves me. Sometimes I get sidetracked, but I always come back to this purpose I have found for my life. God has given me gifts suited to this work, and I receive great satisfaction from them. My life is

full, and I'm happy to know I'm doing something worthwhile.

Challenging periods will always be part of my life. There will be times when I will have trouble. I may even fall. But I know that when I do, God will be there to catch me and stay with me as I recover. I'll never be alone again.

But all this focus on me made me feel ill at ease. I shared my feelings with a friend:

This is a bit too much. Although I want to have my say, and although Christian Info Society have asked me for a bunch of articles on mental health and faith, I'm getting embarrassed about so much attention to my personal life. I want to write. I want to educate. I want to help in whatever ways I can to get rid of the stigma. Yet I have to be careful about how I do it. I can see it's going into a direction I don't want it to go.

The trouble has been that I write best from personal experience, and people learn best when they hear from a person's personal experiences. Working on *A Firm Place to Stand*, which is about my life, has made a habit out of writing about myself. But enough has been said already.

I didn't expect the testimonial that came out in the paper today. Quite frankly, I had forgotten about it. I'm going to withdraw another article I had sent them that they haven't yet published.

I hope to start writing articles that are more about other people's experiences, but still show the perspective I write from. This is the mindset I'm trying to adopt. I could be like a columnist, which is what I think Christian Info Society wants. I would describe other people's needs and how we as Christians can meet those needs. Living room can provide inspiration for this. I'm writing this to you because I am embarrassed. I want you to know that I'm not planning on continuing in this vein. My focus has to be far broader than my own life.

EARLY MORNINGS ON THE PATIO

During the period between May and September 2007, I started waking up at four or five in the morning with no desire for further sleep. The night before, I had gone to bed, eager for the promise of precious hours with God that would be waiting for me in the morning.

As soon as I got up, I put on some warm clothing, and went out to the patio with a cup of hot coffee, my Bible, my journal, and a pen.

Sitting in my beloved Muskoka chair with its wide arm rests and built-in leg support was a great way to enjoy the morning air and our expansive garden. As sunrise approached, the birds' delightful chirping filled the air.

Sometimes I witnessed rather interesting things in this garden oasis. One day, a raccoon appeared from out of the dense row of cedars lining the property. I sat very still but became a bit nervous when he started approaching me, coming closer and closer. He seemed to be curious about what I might be doing there.

Another morning, I was amused to see a family of skunks scurrying across the lawn on their way to the safety of their hiding place under the cedars. The mother led the way, three babies following behind, all in a row. Fortunately, they were a distance away and had no interest in me.

I usually spent a couple of hours there, leisurely reading my Bible and writing letters to God in my journal. Sometimes I read from a nonfiction Christian book. As I read and meditated, ideas came to me for discussion topics I could bring to Living Room for the group to explore.

I pulled together problems I might myself be struggling with, Scripture verses, ideas from the many books I read, and things I was learning from my day-to-day life. I discovered many lessons I wanted to pass along. My stomach told me when it was time to have breakfast. No need to worry my mind over the day.

Each morning is like a little holiday. Those peaceful mornings, spent in the presence of God, prepared me for the busy life I led during the day. As I look back from the comfort of the quiet days I now enjoy as an older person, I find it hard to believe how much I crammed into my life: developing the Living Room ministry, building church awareness, writing *A Firm Place to Stand*, giving support to people in crisis, and— not the least—taking care of a household.

The work helped keep the depression that always threatened at bay. In my journal I wrote, "I feel as though I need to keep working to stay well and strong. Can't slow down too much." If I stopped, I was afraid of what would happen to me.

I can see how working so incessantly might be due to hypomania, an elevated mood, a symptom of my bipolar disorder. It was all for a wonderful cause, with God very much a part of it. Yet I felt driven. Peace eluded me. This high activity was simply part of who I was—always wanting to make things happen. When friends told me to spend some time watching TV and relax, I could never accept such a plan. It seemed like such a waste of time.

Despite this, I was able to keep everything intact. As I write this now, I realize how my long early morning quiet times with God made this possible.

SHARING GOD'S LOVE

On September 27, 2007, I journalled the following:

This morning, I feel enveloped with the love of my friends. To think that I'm so loved by them! It's precious to know.

It seems as though I best realize what love is when I'm struggling with depression, when I start doubting my friends' love. It's when I feel bad about myself and am then assured of their love, that I most understand what love truly is.

> *"How great is the love the Father has lavished on us that we should be called children of God, and that is what we are!"* (1 John 3:1)

God's love is a holding us in his arms love. God's love is a holding us close to himself when we cry love. God's love is a forever love. He loves us no matter what we say or do or think, He will stay close to us, no matter what we go through. Though we may feel lonely, we're never alone.

My biggest aim as facilitator of a Living Room support group is to help participants learn about and experience the love of God. It's when hurting people understand how much God loves them that healing can best occur. I know this because this has been my experience.

I have had godly friends stand by me during difficult times, giving me the kind of love that I knew came from God. God worked through them to make himself known.

1 John 4:12 says, *"No one has ever seen God; but if we love one another, God lives in us and his love is made complete in us."* It's through those of us who love God that God reveals himself.

God's love is unfathomable; it's beyond measure. We can only show a part of it, but we can do it with abandon. We need to accept others as Jesus did, using him as our example, following in his footsteps. Jesus loved the poor, the sinners, the sick. He touched the untouchables and his loving touch made them well.

God's commandments that sum up all commandments given in the Bible is to love God with all our heart and soul and strength and to love our neighbor as we love ourselves. God *is* love. If only the whole world could share in this love! What a better place this planet would be!

But we each have a little corner of the world, a little sphere of influence. We have people surrounding us who we can love and help to heal. Let us ask God to help us share his love with them . . . with abandon.

I myself have found healing through how I love others. When I give, I receive.

LOVING THE UNLOVABLE

G.K. Chesterton is quoted talking about "Beauty and the Beast": "Unlovely things must be deeply loved before they become lovable." And isn't that the way in which Christ loves us? "While we were yet sinners, Christ died for us."

And I think of how much I loved my Living Room people and how even the most seemingly unlovable became so very lovable. And in a strange way I came to love the seemingly unlovable even more than those who might seem easier to love. Does that make sense?

I thank God for giving me that love to love with. Such joy it brings with it! The love of God is very present at Living Room. His presence is there and we are free to come before him, totally open, not needing to hide anything, without guilt or shame. At Living Room everyone becomes lovable. What a beautiful thing!"

I believe it was the sharing of what was in our heart that made us love each other so much. When we reveal what's inside us, it doesn't matter how we look or act. It's just very beautiful to know us as we really are.

I have a good friend who is a troubled person, having suffered a lot of abuse as a child. She suffers recurring emotional pain because of this, yet I admire her for the courage she has had to survive. I love her dearly and tell her this often.

Some time ago I told my counselor what it meant to me to tell my friend how very much I love her and how I love to hug her. It gives me a wonderful feeling to do that. She's the sponge and I'm the water, pouring my love into her.

My counselor said something that had never occurred to me before. If I love showing my love to this friend so much, imagine how God must feel when he loves us as much as he does. We can't "... *grasp how wide and long and high and deep is the love of Christ.*" (Ephesians 3:18)

Imagine how good God must feel when he pours his love into us—such broken people—and when we accept that love like a sponge soaking up water. All of us are broken, needy people, thirsty for God's love. Yet it can be so hard to truly own that love.

When we express our love to others, we can remember God and his love, and let that love flow through us to our friends. In the process we ourselves experience God's love.

I believe that leading my Living Room group changed me. I've been thinking about what it is that transformed me and continues transforming me. And I have to say it's my relationship with God, knowing that he loves me. It's love. It's God's love revealed to me by the people in my life. And it's God revealing himself to me when I show my love for others.

The Bible says,

> *"No one has ever seen God, but if we love one another, God lives in us and his love is made complete in us."* (1John 4:12) It also says, *"Everyone who loves has been born of God and knows God."* (1John 4:7b)

We experience God's presence when we love others unconditionally. And this gives great joy and will change us.

WHERE SHOULD I DRAW THE LINE?

From the moment the small ad about the new faith-based Living Room support group for mood disorders was posted in the Burnaby Now, calls started coming in from people wanting to know about it. I ended up talking for a while to quite a few. Stories started spilling out about struggles with their mental health and how their church had responded. Many started coming to the group. Many one-on-one support relationships started that way.

A fair number of troubled individuals also came from my pastor and his sister because they knew I could help people with emotional problems. I often wished that healthy people in our church would also try to help instead of so quickly bringing them to me. During my nine years as facilitator of my group, I helped many work through the crises they were dealing with. But it all took a lot of time.

On January 22, 2007, I prayed about what had happened at church the day before:

"I think I've become the church's resident supporter. Though I'm not complaining, Lord. I like the role. I'm good at it. You made me to do that. Our associate pastor wants to introduce me to a woman who has bipolar disorder. Another person talked of her depression. Yet another friend wants to know how she can help her friend who doesn't want to live anymore."

There were many times throughout my years of leading Living Room when I felt myself dropping into the depression I was so familiar with and dreaded. What lifted me up was when I remembered the boost I received when I tried to help others in some way. I was able to escape my self-absorption and gain energy and peace by reaching out.

Most people need to talk about things they're struggling with. If they know I'm someone who has been there, someone who won't be judgmental, they will open up. It's then that I can truly connect with them. We who want to help them need to present ourselves as the imperfect people we are, with struggles of our own. It's then that we can tell them about how God helps us.

On September 17, 2007, I emailed my pastor:

> I'm coming to realize that I need to set boundaries if I'm
> going to stay well and if I'm going to do all the things I've
> set out to do. But that's so hard to do when people come to
> you with nowhere else to turn. I seem to be doing more
> one-on-one work all the time. It's something I do willingly,
> yet there is only one of me and I have so many
> responsibilities.
>
> A lady called me twice today needing to unload a lot of
> horrific stuff. I don't resent doing that at all. I know that
> the way I listen and respond to these people is helpful to
> them, but this lady wanted to get together with me.
> Doesn't feel she could share the secrets she shared with me
> in a group like Living Room.
>
> I told her I'm too busy this week, but perhaps we could go
> for a walk next week. Trouble is, this is becoming stressful,
> especially since there are so many other things I feel
> pressed to do to serve the bigger picture. Where do I draw
> the line and how do I draw the line?
>
> Somehow I believe there shouldn't be a line where true
> need is concerned. I know you don't believe that, and with
> mental health there is such a huge amount of need. Yet
> there is such a thing as boundaries. People talk about them
> all the time. As a Christian, where should they be?

Later, that same night, I sent another email:

> This lady who called me today so much needed to hear that
> God is still there and that he loves her. She was hungry to
> hear that, and it's so wonderful to have an opportunity to
> help her in her faith. I should never be too busy for
> individuals like this. And I thank God for letting me be

there for her. I will stay in touch with her.

Actually, this work is extremely exciting and I'm feeling less stressed.

But it would be nice if there were more of me.

My pastor's response was a long one, in essence reminding me of how Jesus responded to the many who came to him. He also wrote:

You could set up boundaries, but you have to be careful that boundaries don't become limits you set on what God can do through you. I believe you need to guard yourself when you can. Give yourself time to renew and refresh. Be re-created. That's what Sabbath is all about. But you always need to be open to opportunities God brings your way, knowing that when he does, he will also empower you to be his healing presence in the lives of others.

In a person struggling with an illness like bipolar disorder, moods can greatly affect how one feels about things. And so, I was constantly having to go to my pastor and his sister to process the many ups and downs I went through as I tried my best to serve God in the way I felt called. I valued them greatly. In December 2007, I spent some time reflecting on Philippians 4:6-8.

"Do not be anxious about anything, but in every situation, by prayer and petition, with thanksgiving, present your requests to God. And the peace of God, which transcends all understanding, will guard your hearts and your minds in Christ Jesus.

"Finally, brothers and sisters, whatever is true, whatever is noble, whatever is right, whatever is pure, whatever is

lovely, whatever is admirable—if anything is excellent or praiseworthy—think about such things."

The Scripture reminded me to be thankful, especially for my Christian friends. I see God's goodness shining through them. That's what has given me the brightness in the past while their love has upheld me. I have felt God's love through them and when I think of them I do feel God's peace.

As well, I have found blessings when I support other people, and especially when I see them starting to do well. I sense their pain when they hurt and worry about them. But when they do well, I feel joy. And what a reward that joy is! These people are not a drain on me at all.

> *"Lord God, when I carry others at Living Room, I come to feel your presence, and that's such a huge, beautiful thing. Your love is magnified within me when I share it with others."*

The steady flame that is Living Room is an amazing and mysterious thing. It is God at the centre. It's made of love. It heals.

AND YET ...

November 27, 2007

There have been symptoms of depression lately. It has been hard to do the things I need to do; I've experienced a lot of anxiety and an undercurrent of tearfulness. Yesterday my doctor put me on Prozac. He wants me to take a therapeutic dose and then carry on with a maintenance dose once I'm back to normal.

One thing that has caused me to feel ashamed is that I believe I rely too heavily on my friends. This feeling is probably as bad as it is because of depression's negative thinking. To counteract this, I've tried to cling to God more. If I go to my friends because they love me and I love them, then shouldn't I go to God in the same way? Because he loves me and I love him?

I have been very open with my best friend about what is going on with my feelings and my thoughts. As a result, she is reaching out to me, calling me every day. What a comfort that has been! At a time when I needed to hear it spelled out, she told me she loved me.

I've given myself a break from pushing mental health awareness, allowing time to prepare my heart for Christmas. I'm finding comfort in drawing and painting pictures. My inner child is being fed with the things it needs right now: creativity, peace, and love. I feel a need to spend my recreational time doing quiet, solitary creative activities. Last night I spent the evening drawing an old Dutch street scene while listening to Christmas music by Pavarotti. What a wonderful time I had! Pure peace. I'm rediscovering my childhood love of drawing.

This has upheld me. Sudoku puzzles have also helped me feel content. And the game my husband and I play often, *Ticket to Ride*, has provided a good distraction. These activities have the added advantage of developing brain power.

I don't feel truly depressed, yet there are indicators that suggest things are not the way they should be. There are too many messes around the house that bother me—small messes yet messes I'm having trouble clearing away. I want to, but somehow can't bring myself to actually do it.

I look forward to Living Room this Friday. We'll talk about how Christmas is affecting us this year. I know I won't be the only person having trouble.

This morning, I think I will make a list of all the things I'll need to do in these two weeks before Christmas. Writing them down will help me realize that things aren't nearly as overwhelming as they seem to be . . . And I will try to keep lots of time for me to withdraw from the busyness. Time to read and draw and play.

At times like this I am happy for Living Room. Living Room offers a retreat from the world, a place to be with other people, a place where I can be myself and I don't have to pretend everything is fine when it isn't. Even as a facilitator, I feel this. There is a lot of love in our group—many hugs shared around. Everyone truly cares about each other.

On Friday there were 18 of us present. I talked about how, during my many years of photography, I learned how the focal point of a picture is always on that which has life. No matter how messy, busy, or chaotic the picture, the eye will focus on that which has life—whether it's an animal or person, no matter how small.

We could look on Christmas as a busy chaotic picture with many elements. The card writing, the shopping, the decorating, the parties. But there is one focal point where we can rest our eyes. This focal point is Jesus, the whole reason we are celebrating this holiday. If we can stay focussed on him, we will be able to find peace. The busyness won't bother us so much. In the midst of the chaos is the One who gives life. He is the light of the world. He is love.

CHAPTER EIGHT

FINDING MEANING
2007 – 2008

FINDING MEANING IN A LIFE
WITH BIPOLAR DISORDER

In August 2007, canadianchristianity.com published my article, *Finding Meaning in a Life with Bipolar Disorder*. The first person to comment did not like my view at all, arguing that: "It's bad. It's a defect in our brain functioning. There is no gift from God about it. Mental illness is bad." Such was the attitude of a lot of church goers in those days.

Another comment I felt awful about was from a person who had lost her home and her family and had some pretty mean words about my views. And it made me think: am I being too positive in my approach? I felt dreadful about it, knowing how much suffering there is and the great losses people experience as a result of the illness, even losing their lives because of it.

My own life was turning out well, though I too went through agony for many periods of my adult life. I've been fortunate in every way, but I mustn't overlook the great tragedy of this disease. I shouldn't be too proud of my own positive spirit. I should think about others and grieve for the many who suffer, instead of flaunting my personal good fortune.

I feel for that person who was so angry with me and can't blame her for feeling the way she does.

But on March 3, 2011, years later, I revisited the original article on my blog:

> "Mental illness is not all bad." That's how I began an article about finding meaning in a life with bipolar disorder several years ago. How I regret having written those words today! I know the message I was trying to convey with the

piece, but using those words tend to make it look like I was making light of disorders that I know from experience are serious and cause unbearable pain.

Mental illnesses *are* bad, as some of the comments to this article pointed out. But I also know that we need to adopt a positive and hopeful view, though recognizing the honest truth. Mental illness can be devastating. It causes break-downs of relationships. Many lose the ability to support themselves. And then there's trying to deal with people's misunderstanding . . . the stigma . . .!

Researchers estimate that between 25% and 60% of individuals with bipolar disorder will attempt suicide at least once in their lives and between 4% and 19% will complete suicide. (Goodwin FK, Jamison KR. *Manic-Depressive Illness.* New York: Oxford University Press; 1990.)

Personally, I have found meaning in life. Abundant meaning. But that doesn't take away the suffering mental illness causes me and so many others.

Last year I was very unstable with much rapid cycling when my moods shifted rapidly from low to high. Many times, these shifts would happen within hours, sometimes within days. I never knew how I was going to be. There were sleepless nights and almost total loss of appetite.

Eventually the rapid cycling gave way to solid depression and anxiety. Often I felt riddled with feelings of shame and guilt. I didn't like the needy person I had become.

But I continued spending time with God daily and in between the bad times found joy and comfort as well.

In *New Light on Depression*, the book David B. Biebel, D.Min.

wrote along with Harold G. Koenig, M.D., said,

> Having one's capacity for serenity and joy restored is little compensation for the agony of despair, much less the 'despair beyond despair.' The only true compensation for depression has to do with the sense of purpose and fulfillment that comes from redemptive involvement with others in distress, sharing the comfort we've experienced. This is the true route to joy.

That's so true! I'm now able to give support to others who live with mental illness through Living Room. I can share with others what I've learned about God's unfathomable love. I can offer heart-felt compassion because I understand the pain of depression. That's my compensation.

Paul's words in 2 Corinthians 1:4 hold true for me as I work with Living Room. I praise God *"who comforts us in all our troubles, so that we can comfort those in any trouble with the comfort we ourselves have received."*

This is how I found meaning. This is how I found joy.

UNDERSTANDING PEOPLE WHO DON'T UNDERSTAND

In the fall of 2007, canadianchristianity.com published the article below. It caused a bit of controversy. One person called the article "unethical and unchristian." It felt bad to receive such criticism and I wondered if I had been on the wrong track writing what I did.

However, I later received an email from Neasa Martin, a person working with the Mental Health Commission of Canada. She thanked me:

> "... for such a beautifully written and compassionate piece on stigma and discrimination." She went on to say, "Your story illustrates some of the important principles of effective stigma reduction strategies. Your message so brilliantly blends the values of your faith with the message you wish to convey. I would like to thank you for your immense contribution in building a movement."

I believe we need to go further than just believing that people need to understand *us*. We need to understand *them* as well. That means that we who live with mental illness should also have some empathy for people who are well but need encouragement to grow in their understanding of what mental illness is and isn't.

Here's the article:

> As a person living with bipolar disorder, I used to feel frustrated that so many people do not understand mental illness. I was angry that people didn't even try to empathize. But through writing and educating others, I've learned that the problem does not lie only with healthy people who do not understand. It lies as well with those of us who live with mental illness. We share the onus of making the world a friendlier place for people like us.
>
> I try hard to understand the people who do not yet understand. This helps me educate others on mental health issues, whether through my writing, speaking, or meeting with others.
>
> We who live with mental illness need to go beyond

thinking that others should understand *us*. We need to understand *them* as well. Understanding is a two-way street. All of us should understand *each other*. Those of us with mental illness should empathize with healthy people who need to be encouraged to learn what mental illness is and is not. We need patience to educate them gradually. With help, they will learn, step-by-step, to cut through the stigma that so heavily surrounds mental illness.

We would like to see healthy people put themselves in our place, with empathy. But we with mental illness must also put ourselves in *their* place, to understand why they have so much trouble empathizing. We need to learn how to build empathy where it doesn't exist. And we need patience with those who can't identify with us—not anger or frustration but showing them love in the same way we want to be loved. In this way, we will gradually remove the stigma.

If we believe in ourselves without shame or guilt, others will not be able to hurt us as much with their unsympathetic attitudes. We will learn to ignore snubs and not return them. We will reach out to others who have trouble reaching out to us. We will learn not to internalize the stigma. We will not accept the stigma but will live instead as though it doesn't exist.

I'm fortunate to have a husband who has always supported me. I didn't have to worry about keeping my disorder secret from unsympathetic employers. I had the freedom, ten years ago, to start educating the public by writing about my illness, trying to build empathy and compassion. My church friends gradually learned from me what it means to live with bipolar disorder. Today I enjoy a church environment in which mental health issues are an acceptable topic of conversation. The faith-based mood disorders support group, Living Room, that I started has become a much-loved ministry for my church.

Most people want to feel compassion for others. All they need is to understand our illnesses better. For that to happen, the stigma that causes fear and prevents people from learning must be reduced. And the only way to reduce stigma is to talk openly about these issues. When we talk naturally about mental illness, it's amazing how many people with these problems come out of hiding. Others become more supportive, and suddenly sick people no longer need to suffer alone and in silence.

Though I'm still angry at the stigma, I no longer feel as angry about the misunderstanding. Today I try instead to understand people who don't understand, knowing that they need time to learn. If we educate with patience, one person at a time—loving them as we want to be loved—the world will become a better place.

As the Bible says, "...live in harmony with one another; be sympathetic, love as brothers, be compassionate and humble." (1 Peter 3:8)

And that goes for *all* of us.

100 HUNTLEY STREET

I had always dreamed of having an opportunity to be on the 100 Huntley Street show, believing it would be the ideal place to let Christians know about Living Room and the work I was doing. I was planning to approach them and tell them about my ministry, but they came to me before I even had a chance to go to them!

They had been reading my articles on canadianchristianity.com and wrote to arrange for an interview. October 26th would be the big day.

In August 2007 I wrote a letter to God:

>*"Life is awfully exciting right now. Good stuff, yes, but not exactly peaceful. So, I guess even good stuff can be stormy and stressful. But I know you will be with me through this if I place my trust in you.*

>*"Help me each morning to reach out to you and ask for your help to see me through the day. I don't know what is going to happen as the result of being on 100 Huntley Street. I'm going to become well known, I guess. And I suppose that's what needs to happen if I'm going to do the work you gave me to do. But it's kind of scary, especially with my disorder and sensitivity to stress.*

>*"Lord, please help me to stay well so I can weather the storms that will most likely come, as well as this storm I'm in right now. My latest article on canadianchristianity.com has drawn several comments and brought people to my blog.*

>*"Lord, give me the words you want me to speak. Speak through me. Lord. Let me be a conduit of your love. Help me to take one step at a time. Keep the waves small and help me to trust, no matter how big they become. You can still the storms, no matter what."*

And when the interview was only a week away. I wrote to my blogging pals:

I'm a bit worried because in recent days, when talking about Living Room, my mouth hasn't worked too well. I've found it hard to express what I want to say.

Perhaps I've been too steeped in all this work lately. My son and his wife are creating a Living Room website, a job that requires a lot of input from me. A new Living Room has started in Abbotsford and another is looking into starting up in that same city. I've been working on devotional samples as well. And then there was the book proposal I sent to an agency recently. Also, I get quite a few phone calls from people needing support. Altogether, I've been doing a lot of mental health work.

Despite all that, I spent much of the week preparing.

I prayed:

"God, please help me to focus on what is most important. Help me to see how you are present in all I do. Help me to remember that this is the work you've given me to do, and it's you I follow. It's your work I do. You are doing the real work and I'm only your hands and feet. This is a big job, an important job. But by doing a little bit at a time, much is possible."

Isaiah 42:6-7 spoke to me:

> *I, the Lord, have called you in righteousness;*
> *I will take hold of your hand.*
> *I will keep you and will make you*
> *to be a covenant for the people*
> *and a light for the Gentiles,*
> *to open eyes that are blind,*
> *to free captives from prison*
> *and to release from the dungeon those who sit in darkness.*

I *am* God's servant. He *will* take hold of my hand and help me open eyes that are blind to the truths about mental illness. He will help me free those who are captives in a prison of secrecy and aloneness. He will help me release people from the darkness of depression through the sharing of God's Word and through God's love.

It's a bit confusing. I'm working on two different, though related, areas at the same time. I'm working to help church congregations become more supportive, and I'm working to help people with mental illness find healing through the love of Jesus Christ. I wonder if I'm not trying to do too many things at one time? But by letting God lead, I *can* do one thing at a time, and if he leads me to both, then I must do both.

I've been thinking lately about how I've come to love the people I care for so much and think I know why that is. I spent years writing articles and books for the benefit of people who have illnesses like mine. I wrote with love for people whose faces I could not see. I love them because I know what it is to suffer in the way they do. I wrote with their needs constantly in mind.

Now, with Living Room, I have them with me in flesh and blood and I can't help but love them. I feel very close to them. These are the people I spent so many hours and years thinking about and writing for. The connection with them started years ago. What a gift it is to now have the people I care about close at hand.

The night before the interview, I prayed Psalm 40:9-10

> *I proclaim your saving acts in the great assembly;*
> *I do not seal my lips, Lord, as you know.*
> *I do not hide your righteousness in my heart;*
> *I speak of your faithfulness and your saving help.*
> *I do not conceal your love and your faithfulness*
> *from the great assembly.*

"Please Lord, help me to openly tell of your love and your truth when I'm interviewed tomorrow."

The next day, on October 26th, the 100 Huntley Street crew arrived. Sherien Barsoum, and Greg, the camera man, knocked at the door at 8:30 am. I wrote in my journal as Greg filmed me:

"I'm feeling good today. Happy about all that's happening. Thank you God, for this wonderful opportunity to educate."

AFTER THE INTERVIEW

There is only one way to describe the way I felt the day after the interview. I felt totally blessed, at peace, and joyous. *"How good you are to me Lord. Thank you, thank you."*

100 Huntley Street did so much work to cover my story, especially recording what I had to say about Living Room. And everything went fine. During the taping of the Living Room meeting, I was able to facilitate as though the camera wasn't there. *"Thank you God for how natural I feel when I lead the meetings. I totally feel myself."*

I've been mulling over all the neat things that have been happening at Living room: the number of people that were willing to come out and be shown on camera; one person's enthusiasm and willingness to do devotionals, and her offer to help paint the church.

Another person says that she's better able to cope with bipolar as a result of Living Room. I'm always surprised to hear people express how important Living Room is to them. It happens all the time. Our new member, a counselor, especially praises it.

He says that he really feels God there. When he goes back to work, he'll plan his schedule so that he'll be able to keep coming. *"Thank you so very much, Lord, for Living Room."*

And I'm thinking of the ecard I received from one of the members, thanking me for taking time with her on Friday. She was in desperate need for care, and honestly, it was a privilege to put my arm around her as she cried and was so out of control. Giving a person love at a time like that feels very good.

Amongst other things, Jesus said, *"I was sick and you looked after me."* (Matt 25:36) And *"I tell you the truth, whatever you did for one of the least of these brothers of mine, you did for me."* (Matt 25:40).

Maybe that's why I feel so full and at peace when I care for someone in deep emotional pain. I'm doing it for God. For Jesus.

CHAPTER NINE

A COMPLEX LIFE
2007 – 2008

MOM-IN-LAW'S HEALTH DECLINES

December 11, 2007

My mother-in-law is dying. She sounded so weak when I talked to her last night, like she's just slipping away from us. She would like a blood transfusion to see her through Christmas. Don't know if that's possible or whether that will even be enough.

Such a shame to see this happening to her. She's still so good in every other way, still quilting and reading. Her mind is still a hundred percent.

I'll be so sad to see her gone. She's like my own mother. I looked after her like she was my own. What a loss she'll be!

"God, be with her please. Please give her some time. A transfusion would help. I don't know what to do about her funeral—who her pastor is or anything. Lord, help Wes and me look after her well, in the way she deserves.

"Be with me Lord, in all I need to do in the next while. Help me please to hold together."

December 14, 2007

Mom's body rejected the blood and she will now have to go back for another transfusion. Another try. Another day in Abbotsford. And today we have a Living Room meeting.

"Please God help me to be strong for that. Not that I'm feeling bad right now. I'm not, but I do want to have it all together."

"Help me please God, to do some tidying around the house to make me feel better. And help my friend, C. She was in bed again yesterday. And S. is not doing well again."

But it's Christmas in our house now. And though I haven't had a chance to bake, Wes got some cookies as a gift from his client. I'll bake when I get a chance, maybe this weekend. *"Lord, please let me keep you in my heart. Help me to remember we're celebrating your coming this season."*

December 16, 2007

We had Mom in emergency yesterday to get another transfusion. I hadn't been able to get hold of anyone in the hospital to arrange going to ADC the regular place to get it, so we had an ambulance take her to the hospital. How frustrating this all was. So, we spent the afternoon in Abbottsford and ended up leaving her after 7:00 PM. There was no point in staying. An ambulance was to take her back home.

Wes and I spent a quiet evening doing puzzles together with the tree and with some Christmas music playing.

"Lord God, I've been reading Philippians 4 about not being anxious about anything and presenting my requests to you. Also, that we should think about good things. But it's hard to deal with the uncertainties. I don't feel settled enough to do my baking. Perhaps I could get Wes to help.

"Please be with Mom over the next while and help me to carry on. Help me to think of the good things. Help me to remember to pray—to present my requests to you with thanksgiving."

"Thank you for giving Mother such a caring doctor. Mom told me that he even combed her hair yesterday. This is so neat. It's an image I can't shake. Doctor Kuhn must think a lot of her. Visiting her on a Sunday and combing her hair. Such love expressed!"

"Think about such things," the Bible says.

IN A HOLDING PATTERN

January 2008

After many problems my mother-in-law's condition declined greatly. My husband and I spent her last three weeks by her side at Tabor Home, her care facility, expecting they would be our last days with her.

I found out what it's like to live in a care facility, spending many nights sleeping in a cot in her room and eating there. We had our motorhome in the parking lot for some of that time, Wes and I taking turns sleeping in it. Tabor Home was as good as dying at home. Mom was loved and respected by all the staff. We were very thankful for the care she received.

We were in a holding pattern, taking it a day at a time, with no idea how long our life as we knew it would be at a standstill. The awkward thing was that Tabor Home was 45 minutes away from our home, through some of Vancouver's busiest traffic. We couldn't just pop back and forth. Life was complex, and yet I felt God's presence in a very clear way.

During this time, I had word from 100 Huntley Street that the interview they had done with me would be aired on January 31st. And I thought to myself: What is going to happen once the program is aired? If there are people inspired by it I will need to be ready to help new groups start up. I will need to be ready to give talks if asked. And I should soon hear from the publisher whether or not they will publish *A Firm Place to Stand*. I'm also busy giving support to individuals and keeping up with friends. Life *is* very complex right now.

And yet, I feel God's peace. He is with me. And that is so good.

On February 1st, I read Psalm 23 to Mom, telling her that she was God's sheep and that he was looking after her. I told her that she had been a good mother to me and that I loved being her daughter. She gripped my hand tightly.

"Thank you, God, for this time with her." I'm learning how tough it is to die.

A bit later, Mom got quite lucid, asking if there was someone with her all the time. I told her that I was. She said, "I don't know how to thank you for all you've done for me." "I love to do it, Mother." I couldn't hold back the tears.

On February 6th Mom passed away, safe in the arms of Jesus. For the last few days, she had not responded. She was truly ready to go.

During the open mike session at the funeral, I planned to say some things, celebrating the wonderful person she had been:

I wanted to say how thoughtful Mother was of other people, even as she lay dying. Several times she reminded me to call her sister-in-law to see how she was doing in her fight with cancer. She had me buy a 90th birthday card for her sister and dictated a note for me to write, explaining how things were for her and saying goodbye. When another resident who had not been well came into the room, Mom asked her if she was feeling better.

Although she had a hard time speaking, she said several times, "I just want to thank everybody." This was a lady who was completely other-centered. A grateful lady. She was an inspiration for all whose lives she touched. And at the age of 96, only a few weeks after her last quilting session, she was at peace. She will be missed by the many people who loved her.

I thanked God that I was well. I thanked him for allowing me to have spent Mother's last weeks by her side, knowing that I had done all I could for her. And I pray that he will be with me as I go on to the next chapter of my life.

LIVING ROOM – A CARING COMMUNITY

I hoped that my life would soon be back on track. I had much to do. But returning to normal wouldn't be so easy.

Many emails had come in response to the TV interview and I needed to answer them. There was interest in starting other Living Room groups and interest in finding churches that are supportive to people with mental illness.

I looked forward to the challenge and very much wanted to promote church support in whatever ways I could. I will need to do more writing. I will need to have an info session for church leaders and a workshop for new facilitators.

But on Thursday, February 7th, the day after my mother-in-law died, I had a call from my brother-in-law, telling me that my own mom was in hospital. I think she had been missing me terribly. But I could only do what I could do. Today I have a lot of phone calls to make, funeral arrangements and other things. Tomorrow I'll visit Mom. No Living Room for me tomorrow.

The house is a disaster. So much cleaning up to do. There are papers strewn all over the two tables in the kitchen, boxes of Mom's stuff in three places, a basket of clean clothes and a mountain of dirty laundry in the bedroom. Much phoning and organizing to do today.

"Please be with me Lord as I do one thing at a time, and be with Mom. Help her take comfort in the knowledge that I'll see her tomorrow. Thank you God for the calmness I feel despite everything. Thank you for your peace."

On Saturday, February. 9th I wrote:

Today's the day I will try to respond to all my emails and some phone calls from the 100 Huntley Street interview. This is something I look forward to doing. I want to encourage these people as well as I can. *"Thank you God for this day. Thank you for my wellness—for this strength you give me."*

My co-facilitator called yesterday afternoon to report on how Living Room had gone. There had been 18 people. They ended up splitting into four groups because there were four new people and some big needs.

One of our members had a serious crisis the day before the meeting.

When I told one of my church friends, she decided to drive her to Living Room to make sure she got there. How wonderful to have the support of our church family! And then I learned that another one of our members spent the rest of the afternoon with her and took her to a friend's house to stay the night.

The person who had received all this care called me to say how loved she had felt. She truly felt God's love through all this. Praise God for making Living Room what it is! A caring community!

DEPRESSION – A LONELY PLACE

Depression is a lonely place to be. The disconnectedness we feel must be the worst part of it. We long for someone to reach us through that wall we have around us. We long for love to touch us and bring us out. We long to sense God's presence. We know that God loves us, but we can't feel it. We feel cold and alone. In limbo.

What can we do to re-connect? How can we find help?

At times like this I long for a call from a friend. I long to hear that someone is thinking of me and praying for me. I long to know that someone cares.

I must draw comfort from knowing that many people love me, though I don't feel they can comfort me in the way I need to be comforted. There are precious few I can go to at times like this. I give comfort to many, but few can give it to me. Am I feeling sorry for myself? Perhaps.

I need a friend who will listen to me and just be with me for a while, without making me feel bad about being the way I am. I need a friend who will not tire of sticking with me as I work my way out of the hole I'm in. I need a friend who will love me, no matter how ugly I feel. I need someone I can count on. I need someone who will remind me that God is there.

In his book, *Emotionally Healthy Spirituality*, Peter Scazzero talks about how we need to recognize the uniqueness and separateness of other people and how true relationships "can only exist between two people willing to connect across their differences." How true this is when one person is depressed and the other isn't! What a gulf there is between us at times like that! How can we bridge that gulf? How can we connect?

When I've been with friends who are depressed, I find the best way to be with them is to talk little, allowing for lots of quiet time. We have gone for walks and I encourage them to talk about how they're feeling and respond a bit. But I allow for a comfortable quietness as well. That's the kind of presence I long for from *my* friends as well when *I'm* depressed.

Scazzero writes, "When genuine love is released in a relationship, God's presence is manifest. The separate space between us becomes sacred space." When a friend will spend such comfortable quiet times with me, she cuts through the isolation I feel. What's more, a beautiful intimacy develops between us. And I sense God's presence.

In 1946, as a result of his experiences as an inmate in a concentration camp, Viktor Frankl wrote a book called *Man's Search for Meaning*. Frankl concludes from his experience that a prisoner's psychological reactions are not solely the result of the conditions of his life, but also from the freedom of choice he always has, even in severe suffering. The inner hold a prisoner has on his spiritual self relies on having faith in the future, and that once a prisoner loses that faith, he is doomed.

Frankl quotes Nietzsche: "He who has a *why* to live for can bear with almost any *how*."

We who live with the highs and lows of bipolar disorder can learn from this. We know that we're going to hit depression. It's unavoidable for us. What we need is to create a life for ourselves that is meaningful. During the times we're well we can build purpose into our lives, purpose that will be so important to us that we will hang onto the hope it gives, even during times of depression. We can choose to create a life for ourselves that will be so rewarding that we would not want to lose it, no matter how difficult the struggle becomes.

Personally, I have found meaning in facilitating my group. Now when I get depressed, I try to learn from what I'm going through so that I can share insights with members of the group. I have found that even the bad stuff has value in it, though it may be difficult to see at the time. I know that this is God's work I'm doing and I have faith that he will help me do it, even when things get tough.

Everyone has gifts they can use to create a rich life for themselves, one they would never want to give up. But they have to work on building that kind of a life while they are well.

CHAPTER TEN

EXCITING TIMES
2008

PLANTING NEW GROUPS

At the end of February 2008, I realized that I needed to devote myself more to Living Room. The time was coming that we needed to have an information session and a facilitators workshop. I also needed to start thinking how best to contact the people who had shown an interest in facilitating groups.

Emails started coming in. Eventually, we had a number of groups started or promising to start:

New Life Community Church in Burnaby, BC
Seven Oaks Alliance Church in Abbotsford, BC
Highland Community Church in Abbotsford, BC
Glencairn Mennonite Brethren Church in Kitchener, ON
Surrey Alliance Church is planning a group in April 2008.
On June 24th a group started up in New Zealand.
On September 14th someone in Victoria is planning a group.
My co-facilitator is starting a group at Grandview Chapel in Vancouver.
On October 27th I had an email from Pennsylvania from someone very eager to start a group there.
And someone wants to start a group in Winnipeg.

THE SOIL IS PREPARED

Looking ahead a few years, on February 15, 2011, I was reading in Deuteronomy about Moses telling the Israelites several times, *"The Lord has gone before you."*

I believe the Lord has gone before us as well. The world is so much better prepared to change Christians' attitudes than it was ten years ago when I started raising church awareness. So much is now being written and said about mental illness . . . and Living Room too. People are becoming better informed.

I believe church representatives will now be ready to hear and respond to the call to start a Living Room at their own churches. If we approach a couple of vibrant churches in each community in Greater Vancouver and the Fraser Valley directly, it might work. The soil has been prepared.

"Lord, I pray for all the communities that still need a Living room group. I pray that our goal for a group for each area will come to fruition. This is truly joining you in the work you are already doing here. Lord, let us continue turning to you for help in this effort."

On March 10, 2011, I blogged:

The Global Living Room initiative which is dedicated to giving access to as many people as possible to Living Room groups, now has its own fund set up. We can now accept donations and will have a "donate" button on our website soon. This will mean more freedom to really get to work spreading the word about this form of faith-based Christian support for people with mood disorders.

Two days ago, we set an ambitious goal, but I believe it is within reach. We want to see Living Room in all communities in the Greater Vancouver area and the Fraser Valley by the fall of 2013. At the same time, we will continue reaching out to the world beyond this corner of Canada, encouraging such Christian support in communities elsewhere.

A group started recently in Miami. And another group is close to starting in Atlanta. A young adult group will have its first meeting tomorrow at Simon Fraser University. I had an email from a pastor in Langley, wanting to start a group at his large Pentecostal church.

Please pray for the facilitators of all these groups. Please pray for the many people who could benefit from this faith-based support.

On November 23, 2011, I received the following email:

I live in the Reno area of Nevada, USA. I read about Living Room in the fall issue of BP magazine and it sounds like such a blessing. Is there a locater or something so I can find out if there is a Living Room group already meeting in this area?

I have not been active in a church for more than a year. The bipolar issue was a lot of that. In a dark time, I received advice like "Pull yourself up and stop choosing the luxury of depression."

So, I am very interested in the concept of the living room. I am putting my toe back in the water about church. The one I think I will probably end up being active in, might sponsor a Living Room. It will take time to find one that is a good match for me church wise, and then gain trust and credibility to lead anything there. Maybe it won't take too long a time for this, and I would definitely be interested. So, I will keep up on the website information.

EXCITING TIMES

Coming back to early June 2008, I became quite dizzy with all the excitement of what was happening in my life. It must have been very stressful for a person with bipolar disorder who was at that time of her life not as effectively medicated as I am today in 2024. But God was with me as I wrote in my journals, constantly connecting with him as I journalled and as I lived.

In the early morning of June 2nd, I prayed,

> *"I haven't turned to you nearly enough lately. Have forgotten. It's so hard to remember you're there when I don't see you. Lord, please show me your face. Help me to feel your presence. Help me stay close to you."*

That night, I would be giving a talk for friends at my previous church, Cliff Avenue. I would talk to them about how much God meant to me and what he had done for me. I prayed that I would give my presentation with the same kind of comfort I felt at Living Room.

On that same day I heard that the publicist from Wood Lake, publisher of Riding the Roller Coaster, had arranged for me to do a TV interview a couple of days before the launch of *A Firm Place to Stand*. A couple of days later, I heard that he had pitched me to the new Rafe Mair show.

God was showing his face.

> *"Please help me not to get too overwhelmed. Help me take all this in stride."*

On June 6th, I learned that my testimony, *No Longer Alone in my Struggle with Mood Disorder,* had received second place for a first-person article by the Fellowship of Christian Newspapers.

> *"Dear God, you really should slow down a bit now, give me a chance to adjust to all this. Too much good stuff all at once isn't really a good thing. Please, God, keep me calm."*

God plunked a wonderful topic for the next Living Room into my mind: Matthew 11:28-30, *Come to me you who are weary and burdened . . .* Those verses that had done so much for me in the past.

> *"Lord, please help those who come to be touched through what I say and do. Help me to surrender to you."*

Later, I got together with a friend for coffee, someone I had given a lot of support to. She was so cute in yesterday's email to me. "Wonderful! I can be a support person for you like your other friends are."

I was so glad to hear her say this. We need to support others from a place of humility, making it possible for them to turn around and be supportive to us when *we* need it. Helping others makes us feel strong.

THE KINGDOM OF HEAVEN

In June 2008, I was captivated by a book by Brian McLaren. *The Secret Message of Jesus: Uncovering the Truth that Could Change Everything* helped me consider what Jesus had meant throughout so much of the gospels when he talked about the kingdom of God and the kingdom of heaven—something I had been trying to understand.

One reason for this was that those phrases are so familiar that they had pretty well lost all meaning for me, as they have for so many others. They are words we tend to overlook. Understanding what Jesus meant has been unbelievably hard and it's a mystery why that should be so. I assumed he referred to heaven after we die, because that's what had always been drilled into me from childhood on. And yet, Jesus said, "the kingdom of heaven is *upon us*" and "the kingdom of God is *within us*." Today.

Jesus mentions these phrases over 80 times in the gospels. It's something I felt I needed to try and understand. What I came to understand was that we can start experiencing the kingdom of heaven today by submitting to God's rule—living under his reign—and being the kind of people, he intended us to be.

McLaren's book deals with *Jesus'* message and not "how Jesus fits into this or that systematic theology." I liked that. We need to start with Jesus and not with our man-made religion—not with what we've made out of him. Jesus is the first one we need to listen to.

Many Christians seem to have lost track of what Jesus' message was. They forget that he was a radical, a revolutionary who wanted to change the status quo. He taught forgiveness. He taught us to love our enemies. He taught us not to be judgmental. He ate with fraudulent tax collectors, prostitutes, and the poorest of the poor. He touched untouchable lepers. He preached that love was more important than a long list of man-made laws. He spoke out against hypocrisy.

McLaren said: "What if the religion generally associated with Jesus neither expects, nor trains its adherents to actually live in the way of Jesus?" I could see that we have more to learn about Jesus and his message than the Christian institutions are teaching. Much is overlooked or forgotten.

McLaren: "Jesus emphasized the inward sincerity of the heart, not mere outward conformity. Outward faithfulness to tradition," he said, "can mask inward unfaithfulness toward God. Religious people can become whitewashed tombs." (Matthew 23:27)

In the kingdom of God, "What will count is what is in the heart, not merely what is projected, pretended, or professed."

When Jesus talked about the kingdom of heaven in Matthew 13:24-47, he always likened it to something that has to be hidden before it will grow:

The kingdom of heaven may be compared to a man who sowed good seed . . . a grain of mustard seed . . . leaven that a woman took and hid . . . treasure hidden . . . a merchant in search of fine pearls . . . a net.

According to McLaren: The kingdom of God comes like a "secret hidden in a parable, like a treasure hidden in a field."

For me personally, I came to think that the kingdom of God starts as a seed within us and grows as we learn to be who God intends us to be. There's an element of surprise for us as this growth takes place and we end up amazed at where God brings us and what our lives can become. It starts hidden in our heart and grows outward.

As I read McLaren's book, I was reminded of something I read in *This Beautiful Mess: Practicing the Presence of the Kingdom of God* by Rick McKinley: "Paradoxically, signposts of the kingdom radiate the most beauty when they're planted in the middle of the most mess."

I prayed:

"Dear God, I'm learning to understand and to be able to define your kingdom better and better. It has been a puzzle but an intriguing one. A captivating concept. Now that I'm understanding that the kingdom of heaven starts here and now I feel so encouraged to spread that message. How I would like others to understand what it means to live your way! To experience the kingdom of heaven!"

"God, I love you and I love your ways. I'm thankful that you have led me to a life of abundance, a life overflowing, a life lived for you. Now that I understand more, I want to continue spreading your love."

As I reflect on this in 2024, I can see how the kingdom of God has been part of my life. And I am amazed at where God has taken me and where he continues to lead. How wonderful it is to be a tool in his hands!

On September 10th, 2008. I wrote the following to my blogging pals:

In Matthew 6:25-34, Jesus speaks poetically:

"Therefore, I tell you, do not worry about your life, what you will eat or drink; or about your body, what you will wear. . . Who of you by worrying can add a single hour to his life?" . . . But then Jesus says, *"But seek first his kingdom and his righteousness, and all these things will be given to you as well."*

Jesus is not saying that we will have immunity from the problems of life, but by trusting God instead of ourselves, we will have confidence in spite of it. When we *seek the kingdom of God* we will find purpose, power, and direction. We forget about being anxious. We trust where God is taking us. Through faith, hope and extending God's love to others—as God loves us—we will experience this kingdom of God where God's rule prevails.

MOVING INTO GOD'S PRESENCE

A while ago I was stuck in a pit, feeling dark and ugly. When I talked to my good friend about it, she said to me, "At times like this you need to move into God's Presence."

I know it doesn't sound like anything really that special for someone say, but it worked wonders for me. There's something about the verb "move" that is powerful. At least it was for me that day. To "*move* into his presence" is highly active, much more so than "*being* in his presence." It's up to me to act, to do, to make the move from the depths to the surface. *Yes*, I thought, *just do, Marja.*

I started working on my notecards . . . or maybe it was the bookmarks. When I do that work (or should I call it play?) I feel I'm part of God's kingdom. It's a good, positive thing to be doing. It's colorful; it's satisfying. The work feeds me. And it did again this day. Being creative does that for me.

So . . . if you're feeling somewhat down, why not try to "move into God's presence?" Put on some worship music and putter within that peaceful place full of light. That place where you know you're loved and cared for. That place where you'll give your Father pleasure.

I am living in God's presence when I'm in his kingdom, a place governed by his rule. The kingdom of God is the place where everything that God wants done is done, all things working for good. It is a place where we can share in what God wants to do in the world. It is a place where life is eternal, starting today.

Dallas Willard, in his book, *The Divine Conspiracy: Rediscovering our Hidden Life in God*, quotes a beautiful version of John 3:16:

> "*God's care for humanity was so great that he sent his unique Son among us, so that those who count on him might not lead a futile and failing existence but have the undying life of God himself.*"

So, what can I do to help build God's kingdom? What can I do to make this world a better place today? How can I live fully within an eternal life?

I could live each day as a gift, where even the smallest creative act counts. I could make some more notecards, I could blog, and—oh yes—in between I could and should get my laundry done. I will put on some good music and place myself in the kingdom. I will do something good and wash away the bad.

In the midst of my verge of depression, I had an idea last week. No, it didn't come from me exactly. It was truly planted there by God. Through my quiet time with God, the mission that some of our church members were going on sprang to mind. No reason for that to happen.

Through a bunch of well-led wanderings of the heart and mind, I realized that I wanted to send along some bookmarks I had made. But I didn't have enough. And besides, they were in English. The people in that country would not understand them. I decided to make some up in the Spanish language. How the thought of such a project excited me! It totally kickstarted a livening of the mind, a return to a positive, even elevated, mood.

I worked happily on this for several days, ending up with 340 bookmarks of eleven different designs. My obsession with Living Room was replaced with an obsession for bookmarks. I imagined what the people in this country might need. They don't have ready access to Christian literature. How could I fill their needs? How could I encourage them? As I worked, I felt like a missionary. I felt alive.

I like reading in Genesis how God created the earth and everything in it. I like reading how he saw *"that it was good."* And what joy that must have given him. If creating bookmarks gives me joy, imagine how great his joy must have been!

LAUNCHING A FIRM PLACE

Saturday, July 19, 2008, was the day of the launch for *A Firm Place to Stand.* It would be a party in our spacious garden. That morning, I was reminded of the verses from Psalm 40:1-3 that I had based the book on.

> *I waited patiently for the Lord;*
> *he turned to me and heard my cry.*
> *He lifted me out of the slimy pit,*
> *out of the mud and mire;*
> *he set my feet on a rock*
> *and gave me a firm place to stand.*
> *He put a new song in my mouth,*
> *a hymn of praise to our God.*
> *Many will see and fear the Lord*
> *and put their trust in him.*

"Today is the day I will sing a new song, praying that many will see and fear, and put their trust in you, Lord. Thank you for the wherewithal and the energy to give this party. And thank you for the support of my friends."

It was a challenge to plan what I would say and what I would read from the book. There would be a big mix of people. Some would be Christians and others not at all so. What can I give them? How can I best interest them? What do they need to hear?

In the days before, there were stresses to deal with. There was a possibility that the books might be held up at the border and wouldn't arrive in time. The publisher spent a lot of money to send fifty copies as a rush, hoping that they would at least reach us.

My son Cornelius and his wife Jeannette, the talents behind *Matchbox Creative*, did a wonderful job designing an eblast which I sent out to those I had email addresses for. It announced the book and provided a link to Living Room's new website where copies of the book could be ordered.

I had a huge kick showing the book to my 94-year-old mother and watching as she read what I had written about her. Her eyesight is failing, yet the typesetting was so clear and easy to read that she had no trouble with it. I'll always remember how her eyes travelled across the page, her face intent.

The day after the party, I woke up at 3:30 am, not able to get back to sleep. I was too happy, wondering what I should do with such happiness. Dance? But I mostly sat there . . . feeling that flood of good feelings, not able to do a thing with it.

I could not stop thinking about the great joy the party had given me. I was bubbling over with it. Seventy friends and acquaintances gathered together. The weather was beautiful, the food was great, the garden was full of flowers, and everyone was happy.

There were people who I had supported through hard times.

And it was so neat to have them here for this occasion. So good to see them doing better. People from my church came, from my writer's group, from Living Room, family members, neighbors, and old friends. A couple of people from MDA came as well.

I was fortunate to have lots of help. My daughter-in-law Jeannette, a cook who loves to experiment, made some very interesting appetizers, including dates stuffed with goat cheese. One of my friends made a variety of hot appetizers and sold books for me. And I don't know what I would have done without another friend who made sure the food tables were always well stocked. She was on her feet through the entire event. My husband and two others had worked hard the day before putting up seven canopies. What a lot of support I received!

Now, in the words of a friend, "a new chapter of my life will begin." I will need to promote the book, using it to encourage Christians who have mental health challenges and get the word out about the importance of faith-based support. It's time to get to work, making a further dent in the stigma that exists. My focus, the Christian Church.

September 14, 2008

I heard from someone in Victoria last night, wanting to set up a conference call with me because people in her church are planning to start a Living Room group. And one of the co-facilitators from my own group is planning to start a group of her own in Vancouver. I've been praying for a group there. My prayer is being answered.

There are now five Living Rooms and another four in the planning stages. Thank God! This much-needed ministry is spreading.

Between Living Room and promoting my book it's beginning to look like I have almost a full-time job. As someone who was never able to have a career because of the severity of my disorder, that's a lot for me. I pray that all will go well and that I'll be able to meet all the demands on me.

I'm thankful that I wake up early and have a couple of hours of quiet time to spend with God and reflect before I start the day. That really helps. And I have learned to focus on only one job at a time, not worrying about the big picture but only looking at the portion I'm working on.

Yesterday was a big day. I partnered with MDA in presenting a workshop for a group of new facilitators. So good to have this partnership. Vicki Rogers did a wonderful job of teaching and guiding us through role playing exercises. In the afternoon I had time with the seven facilitators of the Christian groups and we discussed the spiritual aspects of facilitating Living Room.

My own group in Burnaby is starting a Bible study which will meet every Friday that we don't have a regular Living Room meeting. For some of our people, Living Room is like their church. And every church needs to have an opportunity for Bible Study. Delcie Hennig, a member of our church, reported to be a good facilitator, has volunteered to teach the class, so glad we are able to meet this need.

September 24, 2008

At 5 am I had a call from someone wanting to do a pre-interview for a radio show. Things are moving hard and fast.

"Thank you, God, for the opportunities I'm getting to make a difference."

Yesterday I had an invitation to speak to a group of churches in Crescent Beach in October about the stigma towards mental illness in churches and how to fix it. Right up my alley. I just hope that someone will drive me there.

Isaiah 50:4-7 talks about the kind of attitude I'd like to have. "*I have set my face like flint, and I know I will not be put to shame.*"

The Sovereign Lord has given me a well-instructed tongue,
to know the word that sustains the weary.
He wakens me morning by morning,
wakens my ear to listen like one being instructed.
The Sovereign Lord has opened my ears;
I have not been rebellious,
I have not turned away.
I offered my back to those who beat me,
my cheeks to those who pulled out my beard;
I did not hide my face
from mocking and spitting.
Because the Sovereign Lord helps me,
I will not be disgraced.
Therefore have I set my face like flint,
and I know I will not be put to shame.

CHAPTER ELEVEN

DEPRESSION
2008

DEPRESSION LOOMING

September 29, 2008

When you've been doing well for a long time, it's hard to believe that you could ever be depressed again. But with bipolar disorder you're never totally in the clear. It's bound to come back. Here I am with two books published on how to cope with bipolar disorder and how to be strong, and yet depression is looming again.

I feel down, teary, tired, not up to doing very much. I've also been overly worried and negative about things. This is discouraging.

What makes it harder is that my 94-year-old mom isn't doing well. She's terribly confused and did something to the phone so that she can't use speed dial anymore. Last week she got over-wrought, unable to call anyone, feeling isolated and anxious. I think she has forgotten to go down to meals a few times, which means she doesn't get fed. This is not a care facility. The only people looking after her are those who give her a bath twice a week and those who do a bit of cleaning once a week.

So, on top of feeling depressed, I feel stressed, wondering what we will do about Mom.

I'm going to have to simplify my life as much as I can. Re-prioritize a few things. Allow lots of room to try and get some care for Mom. Allow for extra time with her.

When I told my friend that I was into a downward spiral she asked me, "What are you going to do for yourself?" That's a very good question for a supporter to ask. It made me think I need to strategize a bit instead of just complaining and feeling sorry for myself. I need to reach outside myself instead of staying caught within.

> *"I feel so dizzy, Lord. Dizzy with all the things I have to do, though my list should be quite manageable. Yet, I'm having trouble functioning. I feel I need to visit Mom, yet I don't think I'm together enough to drive all the way to White Rock."*

It's odd to see how depression takes hold. Increasingly I've been grabbed by pensive moods. My husband will catch me repeatedly, head in my hands, just thinking. Far away. At church, I go deeply into worship, pulled into prayer.

Gradually I'm pulled under until it becomes hard to actually do anything. I'd rather just sit and wallow in my inner life.

Being aware of this helps. And, again, my friend's question yesterday came to me: "What are you going to do for yourself?" Her suggestion was kind, encouraging me to "do" something that would benefit me and make me feel better. I know that what I need right now is to "do something," instead of lingering in thought.

What helps is to have a beginning and end to my thoughts by writing them down. To stop them from roaming around endlessly in my mind. To bring them out onto paper, perhaps share with a friend.

I've also alerted some friends and they are encouraging me, letting me know they care. That comforts me.

Sometimes I think I'm making much out of nothing. Yet the onset of depression has been a real one. Sharing my fears with others and taking "action" is encouraging me to escape the deep before it totally pulls me under. I need to stay on the surface and be in the world if I'm to do the work I've taken on.

I have a list of things I'd like to do today. Nothing too difficult. Some pleasurable things and some things that are chores. I think I'll be alright. I'm not afraid.

And I know God is with me.

A COMPLEX LIFE

October 7, 2008

I feel a bit like a nun. Have felt like that for quite awhile now, tied to the work I do, paying little attention to the world around me. I never watch TV. Don't keep track of the news—not via radio, TV, or newspaper.

There's an election coming up and I don't have a clue who to vote for. After 36 years as a serious photographer, I've cut photography out of my life. So glad about that, even if it had always given me such joy.

My friends and my church are very important to me though. They're my support system and I stay in close touch with them. Unfortunately, my contact with blogging buddies is slipping. I feel bad about that.

There are so very many things at me and I think that letting so many things slip away is my way of coping. Because I *am* coping. Though I have so many things going on, I don't feel stressed. I've learned to deal with one little thing at a time, shutting everything else out . . . things like cleaning up the kitchen, planning meals, paying bills . . . opening mail, for that matter. I'm finding it's becoming more and more important to write down every little thing I need to do. If I didn't I'm sure I would forget important commitments.

Now I'm up against something else: My mom is in poor shape. She is terribly confused and sleeping most of the time. I'm so happy that I was able to arrange for health support workers to come in and check on her morning and evening. Even then, I had a call this morning that she had—in her confusion—taken all of today's pills yesterday. Was that why she was too weak to even have a shower this morning? I'm sure someone will now administer her medications.

What makes me sad is that Mom is starting to live in the past. My sister visited today and Mom said how much she misses the family. She asked for my dad who died years ago. She's so dreadfully confused. Feeling alone. I want to love her like a mother loves her young child.

But Living Room is coming up this Friday and I'm looking forward to it. We will talk about relationship with God, drawing from *The Shack* and Philippians 2:1-8 for inspiration. If it weren't for Living Room and what it means to me, would I be coping as well as I am?

IN COMPANY WITH JESUS

October 22, 2008 - to my blogging pals:

> I've been spending my time with God in sadness every morning lately. And I wish it were enough for me to simply sit and be in the company of Jesus for comfort. But I so often want to reach out to friends when I feel like this.

God, who I know loves me and who I know should be enough, isn't enough at times like this. I want to talk to people. And so, I now reach out to you.

Having Mom in limbo like this, waiting for a nursing home, not knowing if a good one will come along, is hard. Time in hospital moves slowly for her and I know I need to visit her often to keep her spirits up. Can't phone her and I miss doing that. Visiting her means a 45-minute drive each way.

Living Room is coming up in two days and I've so wanted to talk on the topic of being in the company of Jesus. I want to talk about how he is real and with us and how we can talk to him. And I do feel him with me, but I wish that were enough.

Yet you know, I think sharing this with you is a good thing. I feel Jesus closer in the sharing of him with others. You, my blogging pals, and him, together with me. My support from above and below. I need both. In the reaching out to you here, I am reaching out to him. That's how God works.

October 25, 2008

Yesterday at Living Room we talked about being in the company of Jesus and what that means. Is being in company with Jesus enough? Or do we need people around us to show us Jesus' love in order to truly feel it? I'm not sure I got across what I really wanted to. Don't know how the session went down with people.

When I asked for hands to see where people were mood wise, about half put up their hands for feeling down. I just hope that our discussion helped somehow. I hope it didn't hinder.

One thing I tried to bring out was that what we need is not just the receiving of love. Just as much, we need to share God's love with others. In that giving we receive as well. We are blessed when we give. I hope I got that across.

When we live with love and compassion in our hearts, God is in that. We are then walking with God. We are in the company of Jesus.

I do believe Jesus was with us yesterday, sitting in company at the table with us, helping us with our discussion.

There are so many ways to cope with depression. But although showing our love to each other must be one of the greatest, I seldom see that in lists of coping skills. Why not?

In the sharing time we had the opportunity to share God's love with each other—to show that we cared for each other. This is what filled me with the peace I went home with. It's this that helped me wake up feeling better today. I feel blessed. I feel God was with us.

I hope the others went home feeling similarly blessed.

IS GOD NOT ENOUGH?

November 13, 2008

In my depression, I've struggled with a need for support. I feel bad about burdening friends with my sadness, although I need my friends at times like this. Yet something a blogger said particularly made me feel that perhaps I should not be bothering them. And the question I repeatedly find myself asking is: "Shouldn't God be enough for me?"

What helped was something a friend forwarded to me a few days ago, pointing out the verse at the very centre of the Bible, Psalm 118:8: "*It is better to take refuge in the Lord than to trust man.*" Reading that helps me to lean a little more on God and a little less on my friends.

And yet, when someone commits suicide, their friends are always asking, why didn't they let me know how they were feeling? Yet so few people want to listen to a friend with depression. Is it any wonder that people take their life?

So, they say you need to reach out. Yet it's also not fair to do so. I'm mixed up and don't know if I should believe my advice to others anymore. I even talked to my husband about this and he agrees that yes, this is a problem for which there doesn't seem to be an answer. I'm always here for others who are depressed and do it willingly. People don't have to feel ashamed coming to me. Yet I feel ashamed when I have to go to people, especially after what that blogger said.

I talked to my pastor:

> When I offer myself to people who are depressed, when I am compassionate and I'm fully there for them, I feel God's presence in a huge way. It's a beautiful thing to feel God's presence within the pain, just listening and being with them completely. And it's when we pray together that we can take refuge in the Lord in a very special way. Those prayers are powerful and they don't come from me alone.

> I guess I should learn to pray such prayers for myself, to find refuge in the Lord and not lean on people so much. I've been looking for something in people that can only be found in God. I think that within depression there is a yearning for God to fill us up with his love.

I thought of a friend who is right now in hospital because she found it so hard to live in the world. Having to put on a face, having to act as though well, though she was suffering so much inside. I wish she'd feel that when she's with me she doesn't need to act. I wish she'd feel that she can be real with me. I wish she'd feel that she can share what she's feeling if it would make her feel better.

Feelings and emotions run deep. Trouble is that we can't see emotional pain or imagine it if we haven't been there. As a result, people shrug it off as complaining over nothing. "Look at all you have," or "look how fortunate you are" doesn't cut it with a person in emotional crisis.

People with emotional pain "need to" share it with the friends who love them. People in crisis find relief by sharing with someone who has understanding and compassion. They need to have an opportunity to talk, to let it all out. If they don't, the feelings will fester within and grow worse.

I guess that's what makes Living Room so valuable. It's a place where we have opportunities to talk. A chance to "complain" where we will be understood and accepted.

WORKSHOP ON STIGMA IN THE CHURCH

October 28, 2008

King David wrote:

"When I felt secure, I said, 'I will never be shaken' . . . O Lord, when you favored me, you made my mountain stand firm; but when you hid your face, I was dismayed." (Psalm 30:6-7)

I often feel he must have been bipolar. He knew exactly what it feels like to be doing really well and think your bipolar illness is totally under control, depression never to bother you again, and then to have it hit again. So unthinkable it is when things are good to believe it can happen again. But bipolar disorder does not go away and we are bound to be affected again and again, no matter how good our medications and how balanced a lifestyle we lead.

Nevertheless, God will be with us, even in the tears.

Yesterday evening, after a bad day, I found myself able to do a presentation at a workshop on stigma at Crescent Beach. I spoke eagerly about Living Room to over thirty representatives from five or six churches. There were other presenters from various resource groups. I was happy that we sat in a large circle (around the Christ candle) and I was able to speak sitting down, the way I like to speak.

I so much wanted them to learn what they can do to support people with mood disorders. One would never have known that I was in the middle of a depression. Nothing was going to hold me back. I hope and pray that this will eventually lead to a group in the White Rock/South Surrey area. Several people picked up manuals and bought my book.

One presenter, speaking for the Canadian Mental Health Association (CMHA), told me that she was fighting back tears throughout the evening because she had left her church, not having had support and compassion from them during her post-partum depression. At the end of the evening, we had a good connection. She has my book now and is thinking of trying church again.

Earlier in the day, I visited Mom and got a tiny start at packing up her things in the apartment.

Tomorrow and Thursday I will be attending the 13th Annual Cross-Cultural Mental Health Symposium on *Spirituality and Well Being* at Simon Fraser University. I'm very excited about this. It should be a healthy way to get me out of the ruminating I've been doing.

Some of the topics:

The Vital Importance of Spirituality in Medicine

A Spirituality and End of Life Panel Discussion

Mindfulness, Meditation and Healing: Experiential Workshop

The God-Shaped Void: Spirituality and Addictions 12 Step Programs: Spiritual Awakening and the Path of Recovery

. . . and lots more.

I look forward to this opportunity to learn and be inspired.

> *"For his anger lasts only a moment, but his favor lasts a lifetime; weeping may remain for a night, but rejoicing comes in the morning."* (Psalm 30:5)

A DAY AT A TIME

December 09, 2008

My pastor talked on Sunday about Bill Hybels' book, *Holy Discontent*. He told us that we all have something in the world that we're not happy about. When this becomes a passion and we know that we want to do something about it we will know it's God's calling for us.

I have that holy discontent. I want very much to make a difference in the lives of people with mental health conditions.

I feel called to help and erase the stigma that exists. I would especially like to help the Church to accept people like me better. I want to educate Christians so that they will treat us with compassion and know how to give support.

Yes, I have a holy discontent. Unfortunately, my work has had to be put on hold while I try to just cope with my day-to-day home life, especially Christmas. How I long to be strong enough to pick it up again! I'm working hard to get to that point.

But as a result of depression, it has been hard to motivate myself to do even the basics. I do have good days when I can do some catching up. Yesterday was good. In the evening, after a full day, I sat down and made a list of all the things I will need to do before Christmas.

Christmas will be toned down a lot at our house this year. My dear husband has even told me we don't have to have Christmas at our house this year. We don't *have to* buy a lot of gifts, we don't *have to* send out cards, I don't *have to* bake. That was a very good thing to tell me. It relieved the pressure I felt.

As a result, I'm now doing what I *want to* do, not what I *have to* do. And I *want to* celebrate as well as I can. I *want to* do some baking. I *want to* clean the house and decorate it. I *want to* have a tree. I want this to be a holy time for us.

My friend helped by pointing me to the Psalms to give me support and encouragement. And I read how "*The Lord is the stronghold of my life.*" (Ps 27:1) I cling to words like those and find peace reading them. God will hold me up and give me strength to do the things I need to do. And I know he loves me.

A couple of days ago I played with a baby. Loving that baby broke out good feelings in me. And I could see how I need to live my life out of love. Love for my husband, my friends and family, and for God. I need to stay engaged with them. Feel their love. Return their love.

And I will live one day at a time, doing what is most important. Maybe this is the day I will turn around.

December 12, 2008 – The Living Room Christmas Party:

In spite of the snow that kept a lot of people from attending our party, we had 16 people. It was a wonderful, intimate time. Good food and good visiting. We finished all of Janice's turkey and almost all the stuffing. It was so good. One of our new members told her story about how her relationship with God started and how good he has been to her, despite her depression and MS. We sang all the six Christmas carols I had photocopied. We really got into it, though we didn't have a piano to accompany us. Such a great time!

My motivation is pretty good right now, though I'm still struggling with symptoms of depression. Negative thinking was a serious problem last night and then I woke up with it as well.

I guess everyone has things they could be sad and negative about. Thing is, you don't need to dwell on them. I've learned that doing instead of thinking builds positive feelings. Trying to build into other people's lives takes the focus away from myself. I then have a purpose that I can live for. And that's where true joy comes from. At least that's the way it is for me most of the time. In an email to my friend, I sorted through these things, reminding myself of what I've known for so long. But how easily I forget.

Today's Christmas party was a good place for me to leave my negative thinking behind. I love my friends there and it was just very good to be together. To do instead of think.

CHAPTER TWELVE

LIVING ROOM PLANS
2009

GOD'S PLANS FOR US

January 5, 2009, a blogpost:

My pastor's sermon yesterday inspired me greatly. I've just come off a rollercoaster of ups and downs and am not even absolutely sure whether I'm off it yet. There were times I didn't want to live anymore, times when I called the crisis line and a prayer line in the middle of the night. Yet this sermon spoke to me, helping me realize it may not all be for nothing. It helped me realize that God is there with me in the middle of it all and that this is all part of his plan (not that he made me suffer but knew that I would).

The sermon was based on Jeremiah 29:11, a verse that is loved by many. I know it has often encouraged me:

"For I know the plans I have for you," declares the Lord, "plans to prosper you and not to harm you, plans to give you hope and a future."

But taken in context, the way Bible verses need to be considered, these words might not be saying what we think them to say. We should realize that God is speaking to the Jews in exile in Babylon. Their lives are in turmoil and they think life is hopeless. Verse 10, the verse prior to this one says:

"This is what the Lord says: 'When seventy years are completed for Babylon, I will come to you and fulfill my gracious promise to bring you back to this place.'"

So . . . God does not necessarily promise our welfare immediately. When we're in pain, or in exile, we may not experience God's promise anytime soon. It may not even happen in our lifetime! Yet verses 12 to 13 tell us:

191

". . . you will call upon me and come and pray to me, and I will listen to you. You will seek me and find me when you seek me with all your heart. 'I will be found by you,' declares the Lord, 'and will bring you back from captivity.'"

God is at work. He is with us in the middle of any pain we might be facing. And how we live our life, as hard as it might be, will affect future generations. The future God has planned for us extends beyond our own lifetime. Even Moses, and many others with strong faith did not see God's plans fulfilled in their lifetime. But their work helped future generations.

Personally, I'm just excited that I can be doing something today to make tomorrow's world a better place. I know how hard it is to overcome the stigma attached to mental illness. I realize that it may never happen. But to think that things might be different for the next generation! To think that how I live my life today might help future generations! I don't have to give up fighting for this because I can't see the results. Every little thing I do to work towards this will count for the future. My pastor said, "The future is bigger than your lifetime. You can do something with your life that is bigger than your wildest dreams." The way I see it, God can do it and we can be his hands and feet.

Now isn't that thought encouraging?

On January 26, 2009, I wrote to a friend:

I was glad to have had prayers for Living Room's future at the leadership meeting last night, glad to have had the support. I felt that it was important to get help "before things get out of hand." I get so overwhelmed at times.

On this day alone, so many things happened.

I went to an Education Night on Women's Mental Health and Addictions put on at UBC Robson Square and did some good networking. I was quite amazed at how many people recognize my name—even Victoria Maxwell, who is herself very famous.

Met a lady who I'd corresponded with who wants to start a Living Room in Mission.

At the end of the evening, I joined in a discussion with a professor from UBC. I told her that I had written a couple of books on living with bipolar disorder. She said, "Are you the one who has a faith-based group? I was hoping I'd meet you." Apparently a colleague or student of hers is doing a study on faith and mental illness.

People are getting to know about my work. It's starting to snowball.

A reporter for Christian Newsweek and BC Christian News wanted to interview me about something, though not about Living Room.

A friend talked to someone from CMHA about Living Room and this person wanted me to call her.

LIVING ROOM'S MISSION

February 5, 2009

Steve Thiessen from Communitas, John Konrad, and Lorraine from the Abbotsford group, Di Hilstad from BPAC and I met. We scheduled a meeting for a group of us to get together to create a Mission statement.

Steve quoted: Proverbs 29:18: "*Where there is no vision [no revelation of God and his word], the people are unrestrained; but happy and blessed is he who keeps the law [of God].*"

I wrote to my pastor:

> Mark 4:26-29 The parable of the growing seed. This is what the kingdom of God is like. Jesus talks about the soil producing grain. Then when the grain is ripe, the farmer takes a sickle to it because the harvest has come.
>
> BPAC has provided wonderful soil for the seeds of Living Room to grow. We could not have grown the way we have without that. I now believe it's time for the harvest. The people I met with today will be wonderful support for me. Each is almost as passionate as I am about Living Room.
>
> Steve wants Communitas to be a partner of Living Room (not taking it under its umbrella). He believes that Living Room should partner with other interested Christian organizations that are interested in mental health.
>
> Each of the people I met with today will be another seed to multiply the Living Room movement. Each of them are strong, capable, smart, sensitive people with influence and experience. Each is committed to seeing Living Room grow. I'm very grateful for them.
>
> Communitas can be another field, providing soil for more growth. That's how I see it.
>
> We talked about Living Room's similarities to how AA developed. I think there's much we can learn from how that organization spread. We all agreed that Living Room is a movement and that it should not be an institution. (again, drawing from the AA model) Not organized with

managers, and without a governing body. There would only be organization to carry the message, produce publications, etc.

"The church thrives where people are focused on Jesus, not the church." – Jake Colsen

I told my pastor how important I felt it was for Living Room to have its wings—to be a movement like AA, not an institution. How it should be Christ centered first of all, even though one or two secular groups, like MDA, might be a part of it. I didn't feel that policing should take place.

I wanted to have BPAC in a partnership position. I hoped that as captain of this movement, I could continue getting guidance and support from my pastor even if Living Room's official relationship with BPAC changed a bit. Things wouldn't be much different than they are now, but there would be greater opportunities for Living Room to grow.

As I showed myself trying to pull away, I felt a coolness from my pastor. He did not believe I would be strong enough to hold my own in a group of strong leaders. It hurt to see him upset with me.

But what if something happened to me and I died? What would happen to Living Room? I doubted that BPAC would be able to carry the ball. They don't have anyone who is passionate about mental health issues. We have to reach outside the church. We have to have people who will commit themselves to the work. I thought about my own commitment. I'm giving my life to it.

"Please, God, help me to be patient with my pastor and to respect his feelings. Help our minds to come together on this.

In any case, we will take this one step at a time, allowing you to lead."

Today, in 2024, I'm looking back at the above and realize what I had meant all along when I asked for Living Room to have its wings. What I had tried to say was that Living Room should be freed, not being a ministry belonging to any person, any particular church, or institution, but "to be a movement like AA. Christ-centered first of all . . . I didn't feel that policing should take place." Such a Living Room belongs to God alone. It's part of his kingdom—he and his Son being the foundation on which it stands.

It's clear to me today that Living Room is not just a group as I had first thought, but that it should live freely within the hearts of all those who love God and want to pass that love along to those who hunger for it, especially those who are being rejected by the world. And Jesus has to be held up as our model.

QUIET TIMES IN NATURE

July 18, 2009

I've come to love the outdoors more than I ever have before. I was always an indoors kind of person, but with the good weather, I've started sitting on our patio early every morning, even before I get dressed. Here I sit for a couple of hours, starting around 6 am (sometimes earlier), with my coffee, journal, and Bible.

So many times, in my small group, I've expressed a desire to feel God's presence. I've struggled often with it. Now I've found that sitting quietly in the midst of nature, fully aware, helps me to feel his presence. I feel at peace.

On our last holiday with the motorhome, we stayed at a lake in an out of the way place, 26 kilometers away from a major road. Very few people live there and only occasional cars or logging trucks passed by on the gravel road. There was only one other party camped at the lake and they were at the far end of the campground. We didn't even get to meet them.

One afternoon, while my husband was out in his boat, catching many fish (it's a very good lake for that), I was sitting in my comfy chair reading a fluff book.

The air was clean and warm with enough of a breeze to keep the mosquitoes away. Not too warm either, just comfortable. I listened to the sound of the many birds in the trees and bushes around me, feeling at one with nature. I felt God's presence.

At one point I looked down at my left hand as it held the book and, at the base of my thumb, noticed a tiny, pale blue butterfly with dotted wings. I sat very still and it stayed there for a bit. Then it moved to my forearm. Then to the front of my T-shirt. Finally, after this little visit it flew away. I was delighted, even more feeling united with nature, united with God.

There's something wonderful and magical when a butterfly lands on you, and immediately you find yourself filled with a sense of joy and a feeling of awe.

> "Happiness is a butterfly. Which when pursued is always just beyond your grasp, but which, if you will sit down quietly, may alight upon you." (Nathaniel Hawthorne)

Indeed, it's a hundred times more awesome to have a butterfly land on you than having to chase after it and catch it.

My husband doesn't believe in God and he cynically said, "Do you believe God told that butterfly to come to you?" But no, that's not it at all. It's just that I sensed God's presence in it and the rest of all nature that surrounded me that day. God was in the trees and in the birds and in the breeze. He was in the warm sunshine. He was in the butterfly. And I became part of all that. God was in me too.

Our time at that lake was so absolutely quiet. The bees and insects were the most notable sounds. And that humming came to sound almost as good as the songs of the birds. The bees did not bother us and we saw only the occasional mosquito. Lots of damselflies and a variety of butterflies.

Oh yes, I guess we were a couple of times surrounded by cows. And their munching on the grasses was very noisy. And they did crash around a lot in the trees behind our site. But a little dog belonging to a neighboring camper chased them away when they became a nuisance.

THE PAIN OF SUICIDE

On September 9, 2009, I gave a talk to a group of 24 people who had lost loved ones to suicide. I had been asked to tell about my experiences of not wanting to live anymore. They hoped to learn more about what the people they loved had gone through to make them end their life.

I suggested we all sit in a big circle to best facilitate good connection between us. I spoke well, telling them what it's like to live with bipolar disorder and what it's like to be so depressed to want to die. I shared honestly, transparently.

In the morning at church, I had prayed over this meeting. I prayed that God would help me share his love. And he did that for me.

Although this was a secular group I did tell the group a bit about my faith and how it helps me to survive. About how I need God. How could I not? But I did not dwell on it too much. We needed to address their feelings more than anything.

One by one, each member of the group shared their stories of pain at losing someone close to them to suicide. It was an emotionally charged time lasting three hours. There were many tears and I so deeply felt their grief. The next day, I still felt the emotions they left me with.

They were grateful to me for sharing and I was maybe even more grateful to them for their sharing. I needed to hear and see the kind of pain they were suffering because I myself have considered suicide at times. I needed to see how their lives were forever changed by their losses. And I don't want to do that to the people I love.

> *"God, please help me not to be so self-centered when I'm depressed that I forget the pain I could cause those who love me to suffer. Though it may be hard, help me to remember that people do love me, even though my depression might tell me they don't."*

I prayed for God's presence last night and he *was* there. His love was there in that circle. He was among us.

I learned that most of us don't realize just how much we're loved. And how we can't feel that when we're depressed and our perspective is off. Even when we're told that we are loved, we tend not to believe it. We can't take it in.

And yet the love I saw expressed by those people gathered to talk about the children, spouses, and parents they lost showed me how deeply the people who took their life were loved. The people who died might not even have realized it. What a tragedy!

And the people in the circle probably didn't even realize how very deeply they loved. They didn't realize how much pain they could suffer.

I think we love our family and friends far more deeply than we realize. When we're busy with our lives and there is so much to distract us from remembering our appreciation for each other, we start taking each other for granted. We forget to let the people close to us know how much we love them. And we so need to do that.

Let us love God and one another—God's greatest commandment, and for good reason.

One person who was in the circle wrote me afterwards:

> I wanted to tell you that my father wasn't open about his illness. In fact, he hid it from most of the family. He wasn't honest with his doctors, therapists, or my mom for that matter. He would change his medication and sometimes just stop taking it because he was "feeling better." I think he never really made the connection that it was the medication that was making him feel better and that he should continue taking it.
>
> Listening to you last night and how you explained that sometimes, in the moment of depression you were thinking of no one other than yourself, brought temporary comfort.

Kind of like a validation that my dad was thinking of himself and not the pain he was about to inflict upon people who love him so much.

I know he had thoughts that we would be better off without him. Nothing could be further from the truth. I am forever changed by his decision to leave us. I have never in my life ever wanted to change something so badly. The pain is unbearable, yet at the same time it's my four young children that have kept me going. If it weren't for them, I truly believe I would be grieving differently.

As you have found support and guidance in your faith, I have found it in the faces of my four young children, and I couldn't be more blessed to have them in my life.

Few people understand what a person with depression goes through. Many don't want to hear about it. So often I've heard from people who had loved ones die by suicide say, "If he/she could only have told me! If only I'd known!" Yet before the actual act, the average person doesn't seem to want to know.

In the end, it's only Jesus who has true compassion. Only he truly understands. And we so need to stay close to him! We need to keep the communication between ourselves and him open.

CHRIST-CENTERED

The team with whom I met to discuss the Vision and Mission statements of Living Room, did not feel as strongly as I did about the ministry being a Christ-centered one. They felt that there would be people in the community who would not be able to relate and be left out if that approach were taken.

September 19, 2009, my email to the team, in part:

I so understand where you're coming from and what you desire for Living Room, but the simplest way I could explain my reason for going the evangelical route is that we have to speak their language if they're going to listen and understand.

The reason I wrote *A Firm Place to Stand* was because I wanted to talk about how God helped me find meaning in my life with bipolar disorder. But probably the biggest thing that motivated me to write was because I wanted to speak to evangelicals. To me, they appear to harbor some of the worst stigma. At least it appears so in what I have heard and in the reading I've done. I want to meet them where they are. I want to speak to them in a way they will understand.

I want to speak truth as Jesus spoke truth in his day. I want to help them love in the way God wants us to love. So many of them have forgotten Christ's teachings and example. They have forgotten what it is to follow Jesus. They've become judgmental. Jesus wasn't judgmental. He himself said *"I did not come to judge the world, but I came to save it."* So many Christians love their neighbor when they can understand them or when they're not too different. But that's as far as it goes. They forgot what Jesus taught them and yet they want to do good. They just don't know how. The world of mental illness has been hidden for so long. It's foreign territory to them.

. . . I've also been thinking how wonderful it would be to have an organization like Communitas rewrite the manual for community purposes, holding onto Christian principles. Now that's an organization I can trust.

Communitas's Steve Thiessen's response:

Thanks for sharing your motivations. I consider it an honor to be able to work together with you on this subject. I have much to learn from you and your experience, and I see you as a "Yeah. Prophetic voice," both in the church and outside on this subject. I think in order for people to get the message that God loves them with their mental illness, we sometimes need to use different words. With some folks they have been so wounded by God language that we need to find other ways to communicate. Sometimes no words at all, but lots of right action.

Anyway, I would really look forward to working together on another version of Living Room. Give us a few weeks though, right now we're pretty busy.

Steve.

John Konrad's response:

I can now appreciate more the perspective you're coming from. I think that for all the years I've worshipped at Highland, and before that in places like Ottawa, many of these issues have disappeared. Your passion for reaching out to those situations or churches where some of these issues have not yet been addressed is commendable and I want to support your efforts in that regard.

Ours could be described more as moving to the margins of the church and taking the message outside the walls and into the community. Both are important. We wish to encourage each other to do what they feel passionate about and feel called to do.

Love and peace, John.

One thing I knew was that I needed to stay true to my calling to help people with mental illness find wellness by sharing the love of Jesus Christ. And by encouraging them in their faith. In the end, I decided that I could never help with the rewriting of the manual. That's not the work God gave me to do.

In 2009, I wrote the following in my journal. It's what I still feel the essence of Living Room should be:

"The basis for the Living Room support model, the foundation on which it rests, is the love of Jesus Christ. Knowledge of his love, the depth of which we try but can never quite grasp, is what we believe is our key to wholeness. We learn to trust God, asking him to fill us with his love and helping us share that love with others. This is how we can bring healing to our lives and to the lives of others."

WALKING A TIGHTROPE

November 25, 2009

My moods continue to go up and down. And when I feel ok, it's as though I'm walking a tightrope, trying to maintain my balance so I don't fall one way or another.

Amazing how many symptoms there are to watch out for. And each time one of those symptoms shows itself, I have to put a different coping mechanism into place, read a different psalm, pray a different prayer.

There are the lonely feelings, the poor eating, overwhelmed feelings where I can't see how I can possibly manage to do the many things I need to do, unable to organize a list. Little things seem like big things. I've even had moments thinking I couldn't go on. Thank God those moments have been brief ones.

Not having my husband home makes all this more difficult. I'm not into a good routine, eat at odd times or don't eat at all. Eat weird stuff, not the kind of meals I'd have if he were home.

Being alone for such long periods means that I often sit for long uninterrupted periods in thought, unaware that I'm doing it. This thinking has often signalled problems for me. When it happens, I need to remember Rudyard Kipling's line in his poem *If.* "*If you can think but don't make thoughts your aim.*"

When that line comes to mind I make the effort to "do" something. It's so important to stay active. The more I sit in thought, the more likely that I'm going to get drawn into depression. I wouldn't call myself depressed right now, but I *am* doing battle with it . . . in many ways.

The Psalms are a good companion right now. Psalms 18, 91, and 40 have been very meaningful to me in the past while.

I'm preparing for Living Room on Friday. Also preparing for the *Into the Light: Transforming Mental Health in Canada* conference coming up this Sunday, Monday, and Tuesday.

I will have to walk my tightrope well. Do all the right things.

CHAPTER THIRTEEN

REACHING OUT
2009 – 2010

INTO THE LIGHT CONFERENCE

We had a 4'x8' poster display at the *Into the Light: Transforming Mental Health in Canada* conference at the Hotel Vancouver. This was a national conference put on by the *Mental Health Commission of Canada*, Vancouver Coastal Health, and Simon Fraser University.

It was exciting because it was our first opportunity to highlight the importance of faith to mental well-being at a mainstream national conference—an important opportunity to show what churches have it in their power to do if they only would.

At certain times during the event, I was expected to be at our display to interact with the attendees. I had brochures with me to hand out, as well as manuals available for sale to those who were interested.

Over the past while, I spent time designing the three 24"x36" posters which hung on the board. It was a fun process. In doing it I had to learn to use Microsoft Publisher. It was good to see what I have the "power" to do using this program. This creative work helped me escape the dip in my mood that was threatening.

MY REPORT

DAY ONE - November 29, 2009

> It's been a fabulous day. I had lots of support this morning, A friend drove me out, leaving a surprise snack with a note in my briefcase. John Conrad drove all the way from Abbottsford to help me put up the posters. It was so good to receive that support.

At the 7:30 breakfast meeting, the lady who came to sit next to me happened to be the very person I had told myself I needed to connect with. She is also presenting a poster on spirituality and mental health.

She came all the way from Aberdeen, Scotland to attend. On my other side, a lady came to sit with me who I had met at another conference.

She's from North Vancouver Alliance Church and is starting up a faith-based group in her church starting in January. I wonder if she'll be calling it Living Room too? She wants to visit our group sometime to see how we do things. Everyone at that table is interested in spirituality, and it came into our discussion a lot.

I met Bev Gutray, Executive Director of the CMHA (BC Division) who I haven't seen in years. She asked whether I was still doing faith-based support and started telling me about wanting to feature me in . . . But then we had to move into the hall for the opening ceremonies. I don't know what she had in mind, but I did give her a set of Living Room manuals.

She also mentioned that perhaps we should partner with CMHA. Now that would be good if they would help us with funding. Thing is, what will we gain from the partnership? I'll have to connect some more with her. Would like to have a really good chat with her. She's a very nice lady.

Tonight, at the reception I ended up talking to someone who produces an SFU radio program. He asked me if I would come on his show to do a ten-minute interview. He's very put off by his Catholic upbringing and his mother spiritualized his problem with bipolar. Don't know if he'll remember to follow through with his invitation. He wanted to interview me on the spot with his recorder, but I told him it had been a long day. I wasn't fresh enough.

I'm finding it easy to meet new people here. Everyone wants someone to talk to. Everyone is interested in mental health and what involvement others have. In the opening remarks, they said that this was the biggest mental health conference ever in Canada. Certainly a good place for us to be.

Oh yes. When people come into the ballroom where the posters are, the first one they see is ours. It's right by the entrance and it's the brightest, most colorful display there. I think people are drawn to it.

Tomorrow morning from 10:00 to 10:30 I'll be at our board to answer questions. I'm looking forward to it. And the highlight for me will be the fireside chat with Michael Kirby, the inaugural chair of the Mental Health Commission. He's a guy after my own heart. Hope I'll last that long. It will be between 7:00 and 9:00 PM. Then, on Tuesday morning I need to be ready to go again.

DAY TWO - November 30, 2009

I had another good day. There were enough people to talk with at our presentation to keep me busy for the half hour. Vicki Rogers also came over to help out. I have our brochures attached to the board and quite a few have been taken. Tomorrow, between 10:00 and 10:30, I'll have another chance to interact with people about Living Room.

I ran into a psychologist/writer who I've met before, and she told me she would like me to be involved in a writing project that she and some others from UBC are doing about spirituality and mental health. That should be fun.

I also talked to a psychotherapist who I found out was a Christian. I gave her a Living Room brochure and she said she had heard of Living Room before. I'm getting so much of that nowadays. Word is really getting out. I gave her a bunch of brochures to have in her office. I'm sure she will send clients to us if she thinks they can benefit.

Just before lunch I met someone I know from Communitas and ended up having lunch with him. So, no eating alone, which I had kind of dreaded.

I've also chummed around quite a bit with the person from North Vancouver Alliance Church who wants to start a group. It's been good to get to know her.

I saw J Peachy, the SFU radio broadcaster, at my last session and we decided to do the interview right away. We found a quiet room and managed to do quite a good interview. I didn't have the opportunity to talk about Jesus the revolutionary. He asked mostly about Living Room, wanting to know what motivated me to start it and the service it's providing. I was happy about how it went. It will most likely be aired on December 21st.

In the evening at the fireside chat with Michael Kirby I actually got to be one of the many people at the microphone asking him questions. The evening was kicked off with an interview with Shelagh Rogers, a broadcaster I just love.

This is very much an interactive conference. No just sitting and listening. Lots of opportunity to have your voice heard. So happy about that.

DAY THREE – December 1, 2009

I met lots of interesting people and had the opportunity to talk a lot about Living Room and hand out brochures—not only at the board during my assigned time, but even more in between. I also took quite a few opportunities to speak up at the breakout sessions. Many people have now heard about Living Room and what we're doing. I met someone from Chilliwack who was very interested in hearing about Living Room and would like to set up a group at his church if he could find a partner. It's finding a partner that seems to be the hardest thing.

MDA was supportive throughout. Rennie Hoffman was very kind and encouraging, and Vicki Rogers spent time with me during the interactive sessions at the board. She had a funny, grandiose idea that kept her from sleeping last night. She thought she should try to get me on Oprah. Well, if she could manage that, I'm game. We need to get some groups started in the U.S. I have lots of people from there visiting the Living Room website, but so far none are making plans to actually start something.

I also met the editor of a CMHA online newsletter who I have emailed back and forth with a number of times, but who I've never met face to face. So that was neat. She told me to let her know when the new groups start up so they could announce it. I'll have to send her some kind of press release.

I also had the pleasure of meeting the Executive Directors of the MDA of Ontario, with whom the new Vineland Group will be partnering and the MDA of Manitoba. I hope there would one day be Living Rooms partnering with them as well.

Now it will be time to rest and come down a bit. Prepare for Christmas, which I'm really looking forward to this year, thank God.

My prayer:

"Just thinking, God. I prayed for the kind of confidence Paul had, and you gave it to me during the conference. Such an answer to prayer! Thank you!"

MY NEED TO WRITE

In a promo to his book, *What Good is God?* Philip Yancey said, "For a writer, nothing really counts in life until you put it on paper."

What Yancey said there is so true for me. I've increasingly found that I'm truly a writer. There are very few things that happen to me, very few things I think or feel, that I don't feel compelled to share in emails, articles, books, notecards, blog-posts, or speeches that I write out. I like to send comments to what others have written, and yet so precious few other people do.

I'm constantly puzzled why others don't seem to want to share in the way I do. So much of what I write receives no response. I expressed a point of view via email to a group of members of my church, hoping it would spark some written discussion. But it only brought responses from the pastor and one other person. And when I posted a comment on a church online forum, no one responded.

But I guess not everyone has time for such things. And I guess not everyone is motivated to write letters. I'm learning to understand.

I send many emails to friends and receive great satisfaction and comfort from sharing with them what's in my heart. And yet I wonder, are they getting tired of me? When they see my name in their inbox, do they think to themselves, "Oh no, not another one?"

And yet I can't not write. Each email is a necessity in my mind, though my husband calls it an obsession. Don't know if it is or not. I comfort myself by thinking, "I'm a writer. That's what I do. That's what I need to do. That's what God made me to do." I feel like Yancey feels. Nothing in my life counts until I've written about it.

On August 22, 2009, I sent an email to Philip Yancey, feeling I needed to respond to something he had written. And he wrote back. It shows how we can have a voice that can use opportunities to reach out to individuals who might be able to cause changes to happen. Here's part of the letter I sent to Yancey:

Hello Mr. Yancey,

There's one thing I noted in your book *Soul Survivor* and had always hoped to get around to commenting on. I'd like to take this opportunity. At the bottom of page 39, you wrote, "On the wrong side of what issues does the Church stubbornly plant its feet today? As King used to say, the presence of injustice anywhere is a threat to justice everywhere."

The suffering of people with mental disorders like depression, schizophrenia and bipolar disorder is great and widespread. Yet the Church, for the most part, has turned a blind eye to the problem, not helping, often not recognizing, the medical nature of such illnesses.

Much too often such illnesses are considered to have a spiritual basis. In this modern age, there's still a lot of stigma in the Church surrounding this issue.

In an effort to help understanding grow and to reduce stigma I started Living Room, a faith-based support group three years ago. A network of these is now developing . . . Here they can be truly authentic, freely talking about their mental health problems and their faith. For many, this is the only place where they can be truly open about who they are. They find out they're not alone.

Too many churches are "stubbornly planting their feet on the wrong side of this issue."

I know mental illness is a difficult thing to understand if you haven't experienced it, and I know that's why you've avoided writing about it in your books. But it would be so good if you could familiarize yourself a bit with the problem. Then you could include mental illness more often when you write about suffering. There are so many of us.

Thank you for your time. And thank you for your wonderful books.

Marja Bergen

Yancey's response:

Dear Marja Bergen,

Your letter was a "grace note" of encouragement to me. We writers work in isolation with little idea of the impact of our work. Responses like yours keep me going and I thank you for taking the time and effort to write me.

You're absolutely right, you know. People support and write about what they know, and depression, anxiety, and bipolar disorders are not front-page news like AIDS or even the H1N1 virus. The public has not been educated and destigmatized on those diseases. So thank you for being an advocate for all those silent sufferers and (gently) bringing their suffering to the forefront for those of us who are uninformed.

It's exciting that your Living Room concept is taking off and providing the support that is so lacking. Hopefully the Church at large will see the obvious need and adopt your program as one of its offerings. I appreciate your suggestion on how I personally can become more aware of this group and even become an advocate for them.

As a matter of fact, some years ago my brother was diagnosed with paranoid schizophrenia, so I know a bit of what you express so well. Thank you for the reminder.

Philip Yancey

DREAM FOR A LIVING ROOM MOVEMENT

January 17, 2010

Often lately I've felt overwhelmed. There's my own Living Room group to look after. And then there's the greater, more global Living Room movement that is starting to grow. And yet it's a huge responsibility, especially for someone dealing with such fluctuations in "mood, energy, and thinking." If only I had just one of those responsibilities to deal with. My group or the movement, life would be easier to manage. . . Or would it?

All too often I start thinking everything's up to me alone and I forget that it's God doing the work and I just have to follow along. How comforting when God brings me back. When I remember that, I don't need to be as stressed.

I love my group. I love leading devotional times. I like being there for individuals as they go through struggles. The relationships I develop are priceless. I feel God's presence in the love I share with those people. I could never give up my group or its people.

And I'm committed to seeing more Living Room groups spring up. I want to see many Living Rooms to serve people who need faith-based support. I want to see this movement securely in place to continue long after I'm gone. Because it's a valuable ministry that all Christians with mental health conditions should have access to.

But it was very difficult to do this on my own. I needed help, but no one in my church had the passion it required. I felt I needed to reach beyond my own church for help, but I didn't feel encouraged to do so. It placed a heavy burden on me, a person already struggling with severe problems.

I was reading a chapter in one of Max Lucado's books about "fear of dying." And it occurred to me how I wouldn't be afraid to die. But before I die, I want to build Living Room into something firm and strong.

> *"Oh God, how I would like to build something that carries on after I die.*
> *"Not for the glory, Lord. The glory would be yours. But just to know I played a part in building your kingdom.*
>
> *"Lord, please help me build Living Room into a strong movement that cannot be broken. My plan is to have a meeting with my supporters and discuss Living Room's Vision as a movement. Would they like to be a part of this? Would they like to help with ideas?"*
>
> *"I am placing a foundation stone in Jerusalem. It is firm, a tested stone that is safe to build on."* (Isaiah 28:16)

Jesus is the foundation stone of Living Room. That foundation is firm, a tested and precious cornerstone that is safe to build on.

September 5, 2010, in an email to my pastor:

> I've been wondering how long I'll be able to carry the broader work of Living Room in the way I am. And I wish so much I had someone ready who I'd be able to pass the baton on to if it were to become necessary. But so far there is no one and the weight of it all is pretty heavy at times, especially when I'm struggling in the way I have been.
>
> I just know that Living Room needs and deserves someone much stronger than me. There's so much work to be done and it's so very important!
>
> One thing I would like to devote my time to over the next while is preparing some of the devotionals I've presented over the past five years for other facilitators to use. I'd like to publish them on the Living Room website ready for people to download free of charge. Over the past few years, I've shared a lot of my devotionals with other facilitators. And I've heard from people who'd like to start a group but need to have some idea of what they can do at meetings. This forms another important block to help new groups get going successfully.
>
> So, you see how much work needs to be done and I just hope and pray I find someone who will be prepared to take over the work one day. And I hope and pray I will stabilize soon.

OUTSTANDING VOLUNTEER

On September 13, 2010, I received a call from Bev Gutray, the Executive Director of the CMHA (BC Div), telling me they were honoring me with their Outstanding Community Volunteer Award "for your dedication and com-mitment to creating better understanding and support for people with a mental illness through your work in faith communities. Your establishment of the Living Room, a church-based peer support group for people with depression, anxiety and bipolar disorders is an example of creativity, innovation, and support. You have made the discussion not only okay but safe and supportive in the faith community. THANK-YOU on behalf of the volunteers, staff, and branches of CMHA throughout BC."

To my blogging pals I wrote:

> I've been feeling dazed ever since I heard. It's so humbling to be recognized in this way. So good to know that my work has been noticed and that it is considered important.

> At the dinner they want me to talk about what a difference Living Room has made in my life. How have I been changed by it? How have I changed in the process of helping other people?

> I will have to tell them how I have had to rely on God in a big way. I could not have done the work I've done without receiving strength from him by going to him daily. Living Room is God's work and not my work at all. All I've had to do is be his hands and voice as I followed where he led. It's the only way I could have done the work I've been doing.

NEW LIGHT ON DEPRESSION

One of my favorite books on depression is *New Light on Depression* by Harold G. Koenig, M.D., and David B. Biebel, D. Min. Much of the book deals with depression from a Christian perspective. I think it's Biebel who said,

> ... depression's saving grace is not that it can be conquered but that it puts depressed persons of faith in touch with deeper truths about reality, spirituality, and themselves than might otherwise be known.

(Yes, I think I understand more about life than those for whom life has been easier.)

He goes on to say—and this I can really relate to:

> Having one's capacity for serenity and joy restored is little compensation for the agony of despair, much less the "despair beyond despair." The only true compensation for depression has to do with the sense of purpose and fulfillment that comes from redemptive involvement with others in distress, sharing the comfort we've experienced. This is the true route to joy.

In my own way, I've found a purpose that I probably would not have had, were it not for the effects of bipolar disorder, especially the depression. I've come to think of depression as fodder, something bad out of which good can come. Though I suffer as much as anyone while I'm going through it, at the same time I know it will help me to help others. And I too believe that helping others *is* "the true route to joy." It truly is.

Today, the purpose I found for my struggles, the formation of Living Room, is alive and well.

December 05, 2010 - When a glimmer comes:

As I'm riding on waves of depression, I'm reminded of how important it is to take advantage of the occasional glimmer of light that comes along—those times when I become interested in doing something that might offer a way out.

I felt good about myself a couple of days ago when I managed to bake my husband's favorite cake for his birthday. Then I came across an old recipe for a favorite meal I used to make years ago. I cooked it up for his birthday dinner and had my son and his wife come and share it with us. It made me feel better about myself. Quite a switch from the way I had been feeling.

Stumbling on that old recipe reminded me of a project I started years ago, putting together a collection of our favorite recipes. And, I thought, maybe changing gears will get me out of this funk. Maybe I should pick up that old project again and publish a little cookbook. My 65th birthday is coming up next year. What better way to celebrate than to gather together all my favorite recipes from a lifetime of cooking?

Many years ago, I used to pick up a new project whenever I felt depression coming on. Quite often that was exactly what I needed to get me interested in life again. And two Christmases ago, during a particularly bad time I put together a calendar using my flower photography. That helped make my mood a little less black. Yes, I believe creative projects can do much to help a person through those bad times.

So tonight, after spending half the evening in bed, feeling quite miserable, I got up and started looking through old recipes. I picked out some that needed to go into the book for sure. And I picked out others that I'll have to test again to make sure I want to include them.

What is particularly good about this project is that it will help me get interested in cooking again. And I know for sure that it will make my husband very happy.

Yes, when that glimmer of interest in something comes, we need to take advantage of it. Grab hold of it and do it. Just do it.

Taking up a new creative project has been my coping technique for dealing with depression almost since I first started having mental health problems. It helps to keep my head above water. It gives me a purpose for the day. It's more colorful than the chores I have to do.

This is my third day in an up mood. So good to feel this way! Today I'm baking Stollen, an involved Christmas bread recipe, but I've reserved most of the day for this job.

My husband gave me a wonderful early Christmas present, Brian Doerksen's new CD, *Level Ground*. I believe his songs have in large part been responsible for bringing me up, for encouraging me. How the words speak to me! They are perfect for people who deal with mood disorders. On his website, Brian says,

> Worship is not always about bringing God our best and brightest. Sometimes it's about bringing God our pain and grief. Sometimes it's coming just the way we are! God wants to give us more than permission to feel—he wants to step into the middle of our feelings and be present with us; even in our suffering . . . even in the middle of our emotions. So let the tears flow . . . let the laments be sung, and don't even think about apologizing!

CHAPTER FOURTEEN

A BUSY YEAR
2011

LOOKING BACK AT 2010

January 2, 2011

Wes and I have been looking back over the past year and are seeing what a very bad year it has been for me. So much depression, so many periods of rapid cycling, so many times that both of us have had to cancel out of things because of the way I was. And our relationship threatened as a result.

I can't help but wonder if I lived my life wrong to make all this bad stuff come about. I wonder if things would not have been better if I could have stayed closer to God and trusted him more.

And yet, I do try to stay close to God most of the time. I almost always start my day with him on my mind and talk to him through my journaling.

Friends warned me that Living Room had become too big a part of my life and that Wes needed to hold more importance for me. And when they told me that, I started work making that happen. I worked very hard on it. And now, thanks to some counselling, our relationship has become closer.

Wes said that he has now accepted that he needs to have a role as caregiver for me. But that wasn't nice for me to hear. I don't want to be someone who is so unwell that she needs to be taken care of all the time. I'd rather be strong and be a caregiver myself.

WHERE HAVE OUR VOICES GONE?

2011 became a busy year for me as a mental health advocate, offering quite a few speaking engagements. I welcomed these, even though I was sometimes nervous about it.

On January 7th, Brenda R. invited me to speak to her group in Cloverdale on April 20th, so much so that she offered to pick me up from Burnaby and drive me back home afterwards. Unfortunately, this visit did not end up happening.

On January 9th, Royd H., a supporter from my church, offered to drive me to Langley where I had been asked to visit a group.

On April 8th, I spoke to a group in Abbotsford. I had prayed about the driving, prayed that my talk would not be all about me but about the people I would be sharing with. The talk went better than I had imagined it would. The right words came without effort, God's spirit bubbling out. I think the people there were inspired.

On April 20th, I delivered a speech for Eirana Support Services in Aldergrove at their AGM. There were around sixty representatives there from several Canadian Christian Reformed churches. The organizer told me that most of the people came specifically to hear me. I was so thankful that my son was willing to drive me.

The speech was in three parts: a bit about me and my life; stigma and how damaging it is; and what we as Christians can do to help. I sold eight books and made a pretty strong pitch for Living Room. There were people there who would like to join a group, but no one talked to me about starting one themselves. I prayed that I might have planted some seeds.

What I came away with from this evening is that people are ready to start learning more about mental illness and what they can do to help. Such an eagerness to learn and discuss the topic! And that's so very good to see.

I pray that what I do will encourage others to be open and speak out without feeling shame, so that we can gradually reduce the stigma.

POSTSCRIPT:
. . . Today in 2024, things are quite different, however. My voice is not given a chance to be heard. Nor does it appear do very many others with lived experience get opportunities to speak to the Church from their heart in the way I used to. Professionals speak *about* us instead. Our voices are not listened to the way in the way they were before 2014. The perspectives of people with lived experience appears to be lost. I wrote the following in response:

GIVE US A VOICE OF OUR OWN

Speak up for those who cannot speak for themselves;
ensure justice for those being crushed.
Yes, speak up for the poor and helpless,
and see that they get justice.

Proverbs 31:8-9 NLT

"Speaking for the poor and helpless." Is this what God really means? I think we need to be careful and think about that a little.

Not every oppressed or hurting person needs someone to speak for them all the time. Being voiceless should not be considered a permanent state. With support, the "poor and helpless" can grow in health and in confidence. Perhaps we who live with mental health issues have too many people speaking for us, determining our needs, and not enough of them hearing our voices. Because we do have a voice of our own and we want to be heard.

Too often we're not considered to have enough ability, credibility, and intellect to speak for ourselves. We're not trusted enough to speak with wisdom. But we understand, better than anyone, what our needs are. We understand, better than anyone, what it's like to be discriminated against, and we understand what pain that causes. We want to tell our stories. We want to be understood.

Is it our perceived lack of credibility that keeps us from being listened to? Some forget that for most of us our illnesses affect us episodically. The rest of the time, we're as capable as anyone else to speak our truths.

As Christians who want to promote support for those who live with mental health challenges, why speak for us, when we could speak for ourselves? Why not listen to *our* voices? Being a voice for another suggests an "I know better" attitude that can strip away a person's self-esteem. They lose the confidence to speak for themselves. And they lose an important part of what it means to be human.

We are real people, just like everyone else.

. . . and yet, there will be times when we need our supporters, just like any other person in the world. Please listen to us when we're hurting and let us tell you about our needs. We will need you.

Will you be there?

STEP BY STEP

May 29, 2011

I need to make Philippians 3:12b mine "... *I press on to take hold of that for which Christ Jesus took hold of me.*" And in verse 13: "*Forgetting what is behind and straining toward what is ahead.*"

My devotional planner posed the questions: What is your goal? What do you want to win? Will you gain the prize?

> "*You know what my goal is, Lord. Removing stigma. Christian support for mental illness. But it is a goal which I'm sure won't be reached till future generations. My goal should be to set a firm foundation of better acceptance of people with mental illness. That, thanks to you God, has been started.*

> "*And what do I want to win? I just plain want the pleasure of seeing Christians with mental illness feel less alone, grow in their faith, trust God more, and be supported in love. I want them to grow so that they can, in turn, support other Christians.*

> "*It will be a better world. "Thy kingdom come; thy will be done on earth as it is in heaven.*"

> "*We're not just working for the future. What we're doing is making a better world today, little by little making it better.*

> "*Thank you God, for letting me play a part in this plan of yours to help Christians get behind people with mental illness—to learn to understand them, and to support them in the way Jesus once did.*

"Please God, help me work effectively to this end. Please help me listen for your direction so that many will find healing."

June 26, 2011

"Therefore, my dear brothers, stand firm. Let nothing move you. Always give yourselves fully to the work of the Lord because you know that your labor in the Lord is not in vain." (Corinthians 15:58)

My devotional planner says that the work I do for the Lord will last forever.

"Oh, I pray, Lord, that Living Room and good faith-based support will carry on forever. Help me, dear Lord, to build this to be so strong a movement that it will catch fire. A spark becoming a candle in the dark. Growing to many candles, eventually lighting up all Christendom. I want to join you in that work, Lord.

"I know that the work I do for you, Lord, is not in vain. Even now many are benefiting. Thank you for that, Lord.

"Dear God, help me to do this work with the power and strength that comes from you. With you so much is possible. You have already done more things through me than I could ever have imagined.

"You are a mist that appears for a little while and then vanishes." James 4:14.

"Oh yes, Lord, I will vanish, but I hope and pray that I will have given moisture to quench some of the thirst in the world before I do.

"When I was young, I hoped that I could make a difference in the world. I hoped that I could leave the world a better place when I die. I never imagined I'd be doing what I am now, and I never imagined the relationship I would have with you."

CONNECTIONS COFFEE HOUSE

September 16, 2011

Connections Coffee House, our church's new venture opened last week and this is an exciting time. Almost 20 volunteers from the church have been trained to be baristas. But it's not enough to fill all the shifts that we would like to have open. So quite a number of people are working double duty.

Unfortunately, I'm not able to be one of the volunteers. Given my problems, the work would be a bit too stressful. Actually, it's not so much the stress that's my problem, it's my tremors.

I'm trying in every way possible to be a support though. I've been making notecards and bookmarks to sell. And in between things, I've been knitting dishcloths. I'm also producing a calendar with the title, *"The Awesome Wonder of it All!"* as a fund-raising effort, though at this point I still don't know if the church is going to allow me to use them as a fundraiser.

They don't really like to have a lot of fund-raising going on and are still trying to draw up a policy surrounding that. Very frustrating for me who would just love to use my God-given gifts to help out. But I guess I'll just have to be patient and trust their judgment. I've put in a word on my behalf and am sure they will consider it.

This morning, I woke up with notecards on my mind. I found a site online selling blank cards much more reasonably than I can get them in the store, so I ordered 200. Too outrageously many maybe? Maybe. But that's the mood I'm in.

Then I emailed the Connections team, asking if I couldn't sell notecards at the shop. It would be my donation. All proceeds going to Connections. I just pray they will let me do that.

In the early afternoon I spent some time with God. What could I do to be of help? It occurred to me that with so many people busy at Connections and my pastor and his wife having a missionary family staying with them for two weeks, there was a need for food. People so busy, and possibly tired, could use a hand preparing meals. I could make some soup! I can think of all kinds of people who could use some soup around now.

So now I have a triple batch of hamburger soup simmering on the stove. A huge stock pot full as well as a Dutch oven full. Good thick soup with lots of meat and vegetables. I'll have lots to share.

CHAPTER FIFTEEN

SANCTUARY MENTAL HEALTH MINISTRIES 2011

SANCTUARY'S BEGINNINGS

March 26, 2011

An exciting thing is happening. Dr. Sharon Smith invited me to a brainstorming brunch on how to come alongside churches to help them learn how to be supportive to people with mental illness. Last year, she had wanted me to help the Muslim and Jewish congregations learn to start support groups. It didn't happen, but now she wants to work for Christian congregations more specifically.

The morning of the meeting was an interesting experience. There were ten of us: pastors, people who teach at seminaries, people working in the mental health field. Someone from Tenth Avenue Alliance, someone from First Baptist, United Church people, Catholics. A wide range of backgrounds.

Some of the time I felt quite out of my element. These all being highly educated people and me only having completed grade thirteen, the discussion sometimes went to places I didn't understand. They were professionals. Me not, except for what I've learned from life experience.

Sharon and her friend Caroline, (a chaplain at VST, I believe) are building an organization called Sanctuary Mental Health Ministries, funded by grants and donations. They see Living Room as playing a key role in this organization, and if all goes as planned, will help fund our efforts.

Sharon recognized that the work they're now trying to take up is what I've essentially been trying to do on my own. Yes, all their plans to raise mental health awareness and helping people living with mental illness are truly the things I've tried in my disorganized way to accomplish.

Having these professionals work on these things in an organized way takes a tremendous load off my shoulders. They know how to get the support and the backing.

Although I felt so uneducated next to this lot of people, when it came time to say who I was and what I had been trying to do, I felt confident and was able to speak well. During the break, I found out that some of these people were already well aware of Living Room and its work. So gratifying to hear that.

I think Sharon, Caroline and our Living Room team should be able to work well together. We can help them accomplish the goals they have and they could help us accomplish our goals as they've been developing. I hope that Sharon can attend at least part of one of our meetings soon. I haven't yet had a chance to tell her of our thoughts of having a booth at Missions Fest but feel that this is something that Sanctuary Mental Health Ministries could also be looking at for themselves.

Sharon and I have really hit it off. I love her enthusiasm and energy. And her training in occupational therapy with mentally ill people, together with her master's from Regent and PhD researching mental illness and spirituality, will make her an effective person for this role. She has also had work experience in this field with Vancouver Coastal Health.

On April 6th, 2011, I took Sharon to meet Rennie Hoffman, Executive Director of MDA.

On June 20th, 2011, I had a meeting with Sharon and Caroline. We had lots to talk about. They want me to be on what they call their Vision team, a team that will support them in what they do. I look forward to serving in that way. They may also ask me to tell my story at Regent College when they do a workshop there.

An exciting thing this partnership is. These two professionals are able to broach the problem of stigma in a way I'm not able. However, I'm able to fight stigma in a different way that they're not able to do. We come at the problem from two different perspectives and balance each other out. It's a great arrangement. We're gradually learning how we can best work together.

On October 21, 2011

I remember a time not too many years ago, before I wrote A Firm Place to Stand, before Living Room, when I tried to interest various seminaries in town in having someone speak to their counselling students about mental illness. Nothing happened. There was no interest. Maybe I didn't have the credentials. No clout to have my thoughts seriously considered.

But how things are changing!! On November 9th Sharon Smith will be presenting a three-hour lecture at Regent College in Vancouver on mental health recovery in the Church. Caroline Penhale and I will be speaking as well. I will tell my story and talk about the Living Room support ministry.

Faith communities are more and more starting to see that they have a role to play when one of their congregants struggles with mental illness. And the medical community is more and more starting to recognize that a person's faith plays a big part in their physical and emotional well-being. Sharon and Sanctuary Mental Health Ministries are playing a big role in creating better understanding in both worlds.

"How I welcome these changes!! Thank you, God!!"

On November 11, 2011, I took part in the lecture at Regent College, speaking to upcoming pastors. I told them what it's like to live with bipolar disorder. I described what my life is like now-a-days. As I spoke, I thought, "Can I help them understand? Even a little bit? Enough so that they'll be compassionate towards others who have bipolar disorder? Enough so that they'll know how to offer support?"

The talk went well. I felt exceedingly calm. Not nervous or shaking as I had been the couple of days before the talks. And I knew it was because I was being prayed for. Trouble was—and I feel bad about this—I'm pretty sure I talked far longer than I should have. Sharon ran out of time and at the end had to cram an hour of material into half an hour.

But my presentation at the very end of the lecture, where I talked about Living Room, went much better. I was able to get everything I needed to say into five minutes.

The note I ended on was that it would be so wonderful if the whole Church could be like Living Room. A place where people can be authentic and not have to hide painful things they live with because of shame.

PREPARING FOR MISSIONS FEST, 2012

May 3, 2011

My team, including Royd Hilstad and Louise Loo, had a meeting with Sharon Smith joining us to explain what Sanctuary was trying to do. We all agreed that Living Room needs to be at Missions Fest and needs to register if we're accepted.

On reading Nehemiah, what really stands out is how Nehemiah prayed about all he wanted to do, and it points out to me how much can be accomplished by prayer. I too need to keep praying daily for the strength to do all the work I'm trying to do for God. One day at a time. One prayer at a time, One step at a time. That has become my mantra.

On May 11th, I got word from Wayne Buhler, director of Missions Fest, that Living Room will be allowed a booth this year. This was wonderful news. Such a good way to let people know about faith and mental health and to be available to talk to people.

On July 19th, I had a meeting with Rennie Hoffman from MDA. Without me even having to ask, he offered to pay for half our Missions Fest expenses--$350. MDA is a partner, in the true sense of the word.

September 23, 2011 – writing to my blogging pals:

> I decided to have an open house/craft sale at my home in November for the benefit of the Living Room ministry. We're needing funds to ensure that we will be able to do our work of spreading the Living Room movement and promoting groups everywhere.
>
> I'm encouraged. This month a new group is starting up in Winnipeg and another in Langley. Please pray for Lorna and Jeffrey, the facilitators of these groups.
>
> But we need many more. We need groups available to all people living with mood disorders who want faith-based support. Everyone should have the opportunity to talk freely about their mental health issues and their faith in one place, knowing they will be accepted.
>
> We are at work, preparing for our presence at Missions Fest in January. This will be an opportunity to engage many of

the thousands of Christians who come in discussion about mental health problems and what they can do to offer support. We'll have to work hard to make the most of this opportunity. It will take prayer and some creative planning. Just glad I'm not doing this on my own. Sanctuary Mental Health Ministries will be helping out. They are also planning on doing a seminar at the conference.

But it's costly being at Missions Fest. The booth is expensive. And it costs money to do the display. It will cost money to have materials printed to have available at the booth. I will work hard to create notecards, bookmarks, and framed prints to sell at my fundraising event in November. It's an activity that will help me stay healthy and it's work I love to do.

HUMILITY AND VULNERABILITY

On October 1, 2011, I sent a letter to Living Room facilitators, as well as those who had indicated they might like to start a group sometime. I shared it on my blog, thinking there might be potential leaders who haven't even realized such work might be for them. I wrote the following:

I recently attended the Willow Creek Leadership Summit, a conference featuring some inspiring speakers, each addressing a facet of leadership. Patrick Lencioni and John Dickson had some things to say about "humility" and "vulnerability" that I would like to share with you. These two qualities are important for Living Room facilitators. They can make all the difference between having a so-so support group and a truly vibrant group.

Dickson said that humility is "the noble choice to forgo your status and use your influence for the good of others before yourself . . . Humility is beautiful . . . We are attracted to the great who are humble."

Lencioni told us how we are called to vulnerability, to being real, to being honest about who we are. "That's how we draw people to us."

Isn't it Jesus' amazing humility that draws us to him? Isn't the acceptance he showed to all, the sinners and the outcasts of his day, that makes us love him so much? As followers of Christ, we are called to imitate his humility.

One of my favorite Bible passages is in Philippians 2:6-7

> ". . . in humility consider others better than yourselves . . . Your attitude should be the same as that of Christ Jesus: Who, being in very nature God, did not consider equality with God something to be grasped but made himself nothing, taking the very nature of a servant, being made in human likeness . . . he humbled himself and became obedient to death—even death on a cross!"

Dickson noted how we consider a humble person trustworthy. Through story he showed us how humility can inspire us. And don't we all trust Jesus? And aren't we all inspired by Jesus' great example?

One of my favorite books on leadership is In the Name of Jesus: Reflections on Christian Leadership by Henri Nouwen. I'm tempted to quote long passages from it here, though it's just a small volume. But I'll try to control myself. Nouwen writes:

> When the members of a community of faith cannot truly know and love their shepherd, shepherding quickly

becomes a subtle way of exercising power over others and begins to show authoritarian and dictatorial traits . . . The leadership about which Jesus speaks is of a radically different kind from the leadership offered by the world. It is a servant leadership in which the leader is a vulnerable servant who needs the people as much as they need their leader.

Yes, as facilitators of peer support groups, we have needs in the same way that the people we serve have needs. We should not hide those needs, but be open about them, as we expect group members to be open. We need to model the kind of authenticity we expect others to have. When we as leaders are real and don't hide things, others will follow our example. I try to do that in my own group, and how freeing it is to be able to be myself with them!! How freeing it is not to have to look like I've got it all together!

May God bless you in your work.

What follows is something I wrote about the importance of humility in leadership.

LEADING IN THE NAME OF JESUS

Years ago, when I was training Living Room facilitators, my favourite resource was Henri Nouwen's book, In the Name of Jesus: Reflections on Christian Leadership. Although it was published in 1989, years before Living Room got its start, the book contains wonderful lessons for those leading peer support groups. It would be good for all Christian leaders to read.

Nouwen was a Catholic priest with an interest in using psychology as a means of exploring the human side of faith—something he felt was being overlooked from a pastoral standpoint. The reason I believe many of us may identify with him is because he suffered from depression as so many of us do, making him an ideal person to teach us about faith-based support leadership for people with mental health issues.

One of the greatest dangers in leadership is pride. The desire to look self-assured can cause us to present ourselves as wiser and closer to God than those we lead. Unintentionally we might set ourselves above others in the group. But this is not the kind of leader a peer support group should have. Every member, even the leader, should be a peer—an equal. Humility is of utmost importance.

According to Nouwen, leaders need to show their own woundedness instead of feigning more wholeness than is theirs to show. Says Nouwen: "We are not the givers of life. We are sinful, broken, vulnerable people who need as much care as anyone we care for." (p. 61-62) This is especially true when leading a peer support group. "The servant leader is a vulnerable servant who needs the people as much as they need their leader." (p. 63)

Through modelling vulnerability and candidly revealing pain and insecurities, facilitators can encourage the entire group to do the same. Honestly sharing faith and doubt, hope and despair, joy and sadness with others helps bring members of the group in touch with God. They need to get the message that there's no need for shame.

Most members of Living Room groups have suffered or are suffering. It's this commonality that pulls them together as a group, jointly drawing them closer to Jesus. We learn to fellowship with each other and the suffering Christ.

Jesus is our best example of humility. He was God in human form but he "emptied himself," giving up all claims of the worship that should be due him. He came to earth in the form of a man, tempted to sin as all of us are, eventually to suffer for our sins. In other words, he gave up everything to be a servant.

> "Who, being in very nature God, did not consider equality with God something to be used to his own advantage; rather, he made himself nothing by taking the very nature of a servant, being made in human likeness." (Philippians 2:6-7)

Using Jesus as our example, we too are called to empty ourselves and be servant leaders.

OTHER - CENTEREDNESS

At a recent Living Room meeting, someone talked about how self-consumed she always felt—both when she was depressed and when she was high. And it's so true. We do tend to be that way, though we don't want to be. It seems to be one of the symptoms of bipolar disorder. All we can think of is our pain. Or, in the case of an elevated mood, our grandiose plans.

My husband and friends often tell me that they think I'm too consumed with Living Room work. Sometimes that's all I can talk about. Other times I'm withdrawn, only able to think of how I have failed, of how unworthy I am. I'm wrapped in emotional pain. All I then want to do is to sit and putter at little things, endlessly doing sudoku puzzles. Can't reach outside myself to even clean up a messy kitchen.

Is this tendency something we can avoid so that we can escape depression? From my experience this seems hard to believe.

I'm always reaching outside myself, trying to think of others. But is it enough? Maybe I'm spending too much time analyzing, as my friend often tells me.

Rudyard Kipling, in his poem "If" said, "Think, but don't make thoughts your aim." How I've had to remind myself of that over the years! And, being a writer and philosophizing person, I do spend a lot of time thinking. It's not always bad, yet I've learned that I need to balance the thinking time with doing time.

At another meeting, we carried on in a similar vein. When our tendency is to become self-centered during times of depression or elevated mood, how can we try to start thinking of others at times like that? Is it possible then to become other-centered by thinking of how we can help others with their needs?

I've tried many times. Sometimes I'm able to help my depression improve a bit by putting myself in others' shoes and helping them with their needs. However, the better feelings are usually only temporary, depending on the depth of the depression.

One person at the group who did not have a mood disorder himself, suggested that having a good friend show us how we're thinking too much of ourselves might be the best kind of support we could give.

"But," I responded, "you have to be very careful how you tell a person that. I've been told that by a number of people in the past and it made me feel awful. It made me feel even worse about myself than I did before and deepened my depression." After all, self-centered thinking is not something a person with depression can easily control.

My best support comes from a close friend who does not in so many words tell me that I'm thinking too much about myself. Instead, she helps me search for things that I could do to get me out of my negative thinking pattern. Play a game with my husband, do a Sudoku puzzle, go for a walk with a friend, work on a creative activity.

It takes a very special person to know how to help someone with depression, especially if they haven't themselves experienced it. How hard it must be to understand if you've never been there yourself!!

WHY LIVE?

I wrote the following in 2015 at a time when I was undergoing great suffering. God was with me, helping me write reflections like this as he stayed close to me.

"For none of us lives for ourselves alone, and none of us dies for ourselves alone." (Romans 14:7)

"Why live?" was the question I had in the subject line of an email I sent someone years ago. I had asked the person to remind me why I should live. It was an honest question. I had truly forgotten my reason for living. Deep depression had taken that away.

This might seem like a good question to ask when we see no reason to go on living. However, it could be just as valid a question anytime you need a purpose for your life. Haven't you ever asked, "What is life for anyway?"

Are you in that place? Many are.

The gist of this person's response went something like this: "The reason you live is so that you can give others a reason to live." For me, a person devoted to a ministry of giving support to people with mental health issues, this answer spoke volumes. It clearly showed what God made me to do and what I needed to keep doing.

I don't know what happened to my depression after that. I'm sure it didn't lift immediately, but I had found a focus for my life again. I had found hope. This thoughtful answer from a good friend has stayed with me, reminding me that God has given me life with a purpose. I felt that my life had value.

Joy came with the knowledge that God had given me life for more than just myself. Yes, joy in the midst of the depression. Joy to realize that life is not about me alone. My friend's answer meant a lot . . . To think that I was needed by others!

God had blessed me with a desire to willingly give of myself. It was a gift I valued.

You don't have to do the kind of work I do for this truth to be meaningful. We all have places where we work, live, and play where we're valued. Everyone can be helpful to others. Everyone is needed by the loved ones around them. We're important to our parents, our children, spouses, and friends. We don't live for ourselves alone; we live for the sake of these loved ones too.

Like all good messages, this one is not good for one person alone. It's good for all of us. But it's especially good when we're dealing with depression. Our life is a gift and God has designed a purpose for it. We are loved and we are valued.

If you're feeling in the depths, don't define yourself by how you feel at this moment. A time will come when you find healing and be lifted up, ready to carry on.

NOT FOR OURSELVES ALONE

Everyone with a caring heart can support troubled individuals, especially peers. As I shared before, the Bible says,

> "Praise be to the God and Father of our Lord Jesus Christ, the Father of compassion and the God of all comfort, who comforts us in all our troubles, so that we can comfort those in any trouble with the comfort we ourselves receive from God." (2 Corinthians 1:3-4)

That means that those of you who have experienced mental health challenges could very well be more compassionate in certain situations than those who haven't.

People who have considered suicide, are encouraged to make up a safety plan which they can refer to when it's hard to think clearly and they're considering harming themselves. It would remind them of back-up people they can call—friends, family, or a care provider. In the plan, they include a statement to remind them of their reason for living.

What I wrote in that space was "Not for myself alone," taken from the apostle Paul's words:

> "For none of us lives for ourselves alone, and none of us dies for ourselves alone. If we live, we live for the Lord; and if we die, we die for the Lord. So, whether we live or die, we belong to the Lord." (Romans 14: 7-8)

I first read those verses at a time when I was deeply depressed. They helped me look at what lay beyond my present circumstances—my call to serve God and help others.

As I've said before, helping others, even when we're depressed, could very well be what will lift our spirit. "Other-centeredness" removes the "self-centered" part of depression—that part of depression that's so hard to shake.

The prophet Isaiah wrote the following description of what living beyond ourselves can do for us:

> . . . if you spend yourselves on behalf of the hungry
> and satisfy the needs of the oppressed,
> then your light will rise in the darkness,
> and your night will become like the noonday.
> The Lord will guide you always;
> he will satisfy your needs in a sun-scorched land
> and will strengthen your frame.
> You will be like a well-watered garden,
> like a spring whose waters never fail.

Isaiah 58:10-11

If we pour ourselves out for others, God promises to make us like a well-watered garden. That is, we will receive the water we need for refreshment. But more than that, we will be a spring of water for others that does not fail.

Realizing there are things to live for beyond ourselves gives us purpose. Our life does not have to be a dead-end journey with ourselves the only destination. When we go beyond living for ourselves, life has more color and vitality. By helping others, our own stresses become easier to manage. We take the focus off ourselves.

Consider how amazing Jesus' other-centeredness was. As he suffered on the cross, in excruciating pain, one of the criminals hanging on the cross to one side of him called out, saying,

"Jesus, remember me when you come into your kingdom." Jesus answered him, "Truly I tell you, today you will be with me in paradise." (Luke 23:42-43)

He was in great pain, yet he responded to another's needs. Even as he ended his life on earth, he was an example of other-centeredness. An example for you and me.

If you can relate to some of what I've shared here, you might decide on a change of direction. Maybe you, like me, need to be reminded that we don't live for ourselves alone.

There is a world of people, friends and friends-to-be, those who need you and those who you yourself might need. There's a world out there for you to explore and become a part of. A world to give yourself to—a world with which to share God's love.

CHAPTER SIXTEEN

A ROLLER COASTER LIFE
2011 – 2012

ON A ROLLER COASTER

November 14, 2011- in an email to my pastor, I wrote:

So glad that Wes is for the first time in our lives together, showing an interest in learning more about mood disorders off the Internet. He looked up rapid cycling, which is a form of bipolar I have been experiencing for the last several months. He told me that the way he sees me, the diagnosis he would give me if he were my doctor would be ultra, ultra rapid cycling, extreme highs, going to extreme lows in rapid succession.

I don't know what I would do without God, and sometimes I wonder. Is this actually a gift from him? One thought that came to me this morning was how having moods this is like being a child. Wordsworth wrote, "Sweet, childish days that were as long as 20 days are now." My days are childish days, filled with wonderful and colorful things to do and think and feel. So much crammed into each day that those hours feel like much more than one day.

Like I said, maybe all this *is* from God. When I do go down, he lets me suffer for only a short while. Then he buoys me up again, especially when I connect with another person in some way.

On November 18, 2011, I wrote:

My mood has been going low. I tend to sit on the bed a lot with my thoughts, getting carried away with them. But going to Connections at times when I've been tempted to isolate like this draws me out from within myself. And that's such a wonderful thing. So neat to find people to talk to. People who know my name. People who can take my thoughts to other places, places where *their* lives are.

It was like that last night. I didn't realize the weather was so bad or I might not have gone, but I did get out in spite of it and was blessed. A brief but neat visiting time with a couple of people. Also, a very cute little boy to watch as he played.

I didn't stay long, but was refreshed and came home to Wes, my mood lifted. So nice to have a coffee shop like Connections to go to. God's light in our neighborhood.

I've been traveling through a variety of moods. There were times that I moved very slowly and felt dazed. Yet I was accomplishing things, tidying around the house, working on Missions Fest preparations, jumping from one project to another. There were other times when I came out of this daze and everything felt bright and clear. I functioned normally. In the afternoon, I woke up from a nap, dreading life, almost not wanting to continue. Every once in awhile I felt on the verge of what might be psychosis. All this in one day.

I'm spending a lot of time on the bed. It feels warm and safe there. But despite this messy brain disorder, I do feel that I'm close to God. And that's a comfort. I don't know what I'd do without him.

A couple of days later, I saw my psychiatrist and he looked on what I'm experiencing as a critical thing. There is a danger that the hypomania I've been experiencing, often mixed with depression and suicidal ideations, could turn into mania. And that could go to psychosis.

Later in the appointment, he dropped a bomb shell. He told me that he's retiring at the end of this year. I will have to have another psychiatrist in place by then. Not much time to make new arrangements. And it is especially bad now when I'm in a critical situation. It's going to take all the faith and surrendering to God I have.

Wes has been helping a lot. He has been good to talk to, not minding talk about spiritual things. We have many good discussions. He is supportive in every way he's able. And my counselor was a great help. I may have to see her more often, seeing her once a week was so good. I feel like she's a good friend, even though I have to pay a lot of money to see her.

My psychiatrist said that he feels I should be out of this disorganized state in a couple of weeks if I hang tight on the meds I'm currently on, but it's tough. I keep tossing over all the things I need to do, dazed. Wes catches me, constantly with my head in my hands, appearing to be in another world. But I'm just thinking of a lot of stuff. Not really depressed, just preoccupied.

POSTSCRIPT:
Today, in 2024, as I review my journals I found out some things that I didn't know when I wrote the above. My medications were mismanaged in an extremely bad way. My psychiatrist at the time had me taking 75mg of Loxapine—a massive dose, as my subsequent psychiatrist later informed me. Today I still take Loxapine, but a mere 12.5 mg per day. Of course, I do take other medications as well. And I'm left wondering: To what extent was the mismanagement of my medications responsible for the great struggles I experienced? One thing I know, when a new psychiatrist came onboard with different medications, I stabilized very well.

On December 12, 2011, I sent an email to my team, telling them that I didn't think I should hang onto the leadership in the state I was in.

Is there anything you can do or help me do? I have names of keen Living Room people if you think it would be good to get some help somewhere.

Just so very sorry to be letting people down.

And yet, I know that God is good and that this is his work and I know that all will work out somehow. I also know that through his power all will turn out for the good. I trust him and feel his love, nevertheless.

Please pray for me, and especially for Wes.

I searched for support:

The rapid cycling continued, without proper medication to help me. People who witnessed my behavior lost the respect they used to have for me when I had first started Living Room.

As I suffered, I sent endless emails to two friends to whom I had become attached from the moment I started going to this church. I couldn't help myself. I had never in my life received the godly love they had shown me. They had become like mother and father to me, a person who so very much still had the heart of a child beating within her.

I wrote those many emails, despite the great guilt and shame I felt in doing so, unable to help myself. There were none other like these two dear people in my life with whom I could share what was happening to me. I didn't know where else I could go to in my times of deep darkness, when I wanted to die and I just needed someone to talk to and pray with.

And yet, my journal was full of prayers to God. I never lost my connection with God. I needed both—God, as well as godly people who knew his love. I needed to feel the tangible love of people close to me, as well as a spiritual God whose love was above all.

God is number one in my life. I value my relationship with him. But when dark moods come, I need someone to remind me of his love and trustworthiness. A spiritual weakness of mine? Perhaps. But I know it's a common problem for people with depression. It's all part of the package.

Eventually, I was fortunate enough to be sent to Burnaby Mental Health, where a new psychiatrist was found for me.

FEELING STIGMATIZED

December 1-3, 2011, to my blogging pals:

I had always thought that I had not been touched too much by the effects of stigma. But in the last little while, I've been deeply hurt a number of times by hurtful remarks. One of the worst things is that the remarks were made to me by friends who I had considered supporters.

If it weren't for the friendship of three caring and compassionate people in the church who offer strong support, I might have been tempted to leave this church, though it has done so much to encourage me and Living Room. I had just yesterday lauded the wonderful work of the church in supporting people with mental illness and how that has led to many Living Room groups.

But the poison of the remarks has been more painful than the effects of the disorder itself. They are affecting me deeply. Is it the effects of my severe moods, making me especially sensitive? Never-the-less, it sickens me to have my pain and the pain of others who live with mental illness so badly misunderstood.

What led to this post is something a friend said to me this morning in response to my current problems with rapid cycling. She said "Your husband deserves a medal. Most husbands would have been out of there long ago." She has said almost the same thing a number of times before and it has hurt me deeply.

By saying this she suggests that all I've been to my husband is a drain. That I haven't given him anything. That I don't give anything back. And that is so completely false.

The truth is that I give a lot to my family, my community—even the world. But when she said this it was as though that didn't count for anything. It's as if I'm not thought to be as human as "normal" people. As though the only thing worth looking at is my mental illness. The good things about me are ignored.

As much as I'm able, I pour out all I have in love for others. I pour out until I have almost nothing left to give. Then I have to refresh myself at the never-ending fountain of Jesus' love. I rest; I recover; and then I am ready to start working again. Resting is what I'm trying to do now.

Thing is, I know that I'm worth a bundle to God. He loves me deeply and has blessed me by giving me a big job to do for him. At times I feel too small, even unworthy, to carry such a load. But he has entrusted this work to me and I feel very grateful. Because it's obvious he does think of me as a person of great worth. How humbling that is, and how I need to take care of myself so that I can continue working! How important to rest in him despite the big commitments I have made, in spite of so often feeling overwhelmed!

I need to cast off this pain and ignore people who are so in the dark about the truth! I will pay no attention to this kind of treatment. I will keep my distance from the people who stigmatize me and cause me pain. And when I need to talk with them, I will treat them as warmly as I can, in the way I would want to be treated. Maybe one day they will come around.

I mentioned that there were only three people who support me. But in that dark state I forgot many things. Looking at it today, I can see that there are many people in the church who love me and appreciate me.

Yes, the church as a whole is very supportive. They see me as a worthy human being, worthy of their love. Most members of the church know what I deal with and will openly talk with me about it when we have one-on-one time. And they feel that they can talk with me about their problems too.

No way would I want to leave this church. It offers everything I need and believe in. I thank God for this wonderful Christian community.

A couple of years later, on Sunday, August 11, 2013, I wrote,

I came away from church today feeling all hurt again. After the service I felt lost, in the way it often happens. I felt like no one wanted to talk to me. I felt uncared for, ignored, and it hurt. I wrote my good friend about it. Hope she'll have compassion.

Interesting thing is that my email to her was very similar to emails I receive from people who don't feel at home in their church. They hurt too. They, too, feel like they don't fit in.

"Lord, please help this pain dissolve. I'm hoping for words of love and encouragement from the friend I emailed. But I also need to remember what I am to you. That should be enough for me.

"Oh Lord, help me to embrace your love, to fully believe how amazingly great it is."

And I remember what my pastor wrote to me a while ago. He said, "I love you greatly and I admire you."

That means so much to me.

PLANS FOR THE FUTURE

December 29, 2011 – to my blogging pals

Since I started writing to you, many things have changed for me. I ended up starting a ministry that is reaching far and wide. I'm grateful for how far God has taken Living Room.

Lately though I've been wondering how long I can keep leading this ministry. I've been having a lot of troubles. Loss of memory; disorganization; having normal or high moods followed very quickly by depression, often with suicidal ideation. Not very good for the leader of an important ministry.

And I wonder: Is this the way it's always going to be for me? Is this a permanent condition caused by old age setting in? That is indeed a worry. I need to consider what can be done.

How I would love to find someone to take my place! Someone who I could at least groom to take over leadership from me.

I did hope and pray to have Living Room groups in churches readily available to as many people as possible. I hoped to start a movement toward reaching that goal. That was my prayer, whether voiced or not.

My prayer is that this *will* indeed be a movement that will catch fire. I pray that the Living Room candle that God helped me light will become a blaze of enlightenment in churches everywhere. I pray that all Christians living with mental illness will find themselves able to talk comfortably about their troubles with their church friends. I pray that they will be able to truly be themselves, authentic members of their church families, open about who they are and what they deal with.

I pray for empathy and sympathy, the elimination of feelings of shame. I pray that the Church will be a source of comfort for people dealing with emotional difficulties. And, if the source of the problem is medical, I pray that it will be recognized as such and that the Church will somehow work with medical staff in seeing that needs are met. I also pray that medical staff will work alongside the Church where spiritual help is needed.

Erasing stigma is a long-distance race, one that I will personally not give up fighting as long as I am able. I'm sure I will not see the finish line in my lifetime. But I have faith that with God's help a better life for Christians with mental illness will be possible. In the way God has helped me, God will help others carry the cause to the finish line.

A CREATIVE RESPONSE

January 17, 2012

My devotional planner quotes Job 17:11: *"My days have passed, my plans are shattered, and so are the desires of my heart."*

Job's old life with his plans were shattered—taken away from him. And how I understand his feelings, though my situation isn't nearly as bad. And I do feel in great need of a new project. Something creative, without stress. I believe that if I had a good project to focus on, I would recover much sooner.

Living Room isn't shattered. It can't be. There will, I trust, be others, more capable, to carry it on. It's a movement. What I do grieve is my lack of ability to function in a dependable way. I just pray that I will recover and that God will help me get stronger in that respect.

But any time that I've had mental health problems I've turned to a creative project to "restore my heart" and give me a sense of excitement about life again. This is what I'm exploring now. I would like to create some kind of devotional book, including my photographs. How I would love a project like that!! This is the idea I'm developing now.

The devotional booklet I'm thinking of creating would be a gift book with photographs and words—perhaps prayers that people with all kinds of pain would be able to relate to. How I'd like to be like David, creating psalms that arose from the situations he was in, but not specifying those situations in his writing. The way he wrote was something almost everyone could relate to.

Could I write prayers that could bless people with all different forms of pain and joy? Could I write something for the benefit of many, and not just for myself?

On January 20th, I started to function better, getting quite a few things done around the house. And I was becoming more organized, doing much to prepare for Missions Fest.

During a sermon, I was reminded of how photographing nature is very much an act of worship for me. How I love capturing the beautiful things in nature, especially when I know there will be people to share the results with! It's like a songwriter writing songs to sing for people and with people. Praises to God. Expressions of devotion to him. I would like to be like David writing his psalms, only in photography form. And, if I can express and share my feelings through the photographs I make, all the more meaningful.

Look at how David expressed his myriad emotions with us in his psalms. How they bless us now! When I'm going through hard times, it's the Psalms I go to for comfort. He went through the same things I experience, though his life and circumstances were a lot different. David understood.

One of the things the sermon covered was on how to engage in a "holy waste of time". The pastor said that three practices appear to be a "waste" of time but aren't really: observing the Sabbath, worship, and daily personal time with God.

This so encouraged me. The work God seems to be leading me to include all of these: time in the outdoors, appreciating what God has given us; the making of photographs to sing about the wonders I uncover; the time spent writing prayers on behalf of others who might be experiencing feelings of pain or joy.

MISSIONS FEST, 2012

Monday, January 30, 2012, to my blogging pals:

This past weekend at our Living Room booth was very exciting! So many people stopped by to get information! People with mood disorders, people who had friends or family members with mood disorders. Others were just very happy to see that there is a way that the church is addressing the problem of mental illness.

We heard stories of how the church had totally misunderstood the medical nature of mood disorders and prayed over unconfessed sins in an effort to heal the person. We talked about the pain this causes. We talked about stigma in the Church.

It was great to stand amongst all the other forms of ministries, the first time a mental health ministry was represented at Missions Fest. I felt we gained credibility and really made an impact. I do hope we'll have the opportunity to do this again next year.

And me? How do I feel now? I'm feeling much stronger than I was, looking forward to getting life back on track again.

"Father God, I feel so blessed! Thank you so much for how things went at Missions Fest! So much affirmation that what we were doing is a good thing! So much support from the volunteers who came to work at the booth!"

January 31, 2012 - an email to my Living Room team:

The response to our booth has so very much encouraged me. I can see how great the need is and the desire for groups. For example, there were such a lot of people asking for a group in Surrey. How can we make that happen?

My feelings are so mixed right now. Today I feel I'd like to speak to church groups about my experiences and the need for Living Room groups. I'd like to share how it was for me to start a group.

Last year, I gave a talk to a large group from the Canadian Reformed Church in the Valley. I was able to speak well and at length. Eventually someone heard the call and started the Langley Group. That would not have happened if this person hadn't heard me speak.

I can see how the best way to start new groups would be to give talks at churches. If I only had the opportunity, strength, and stability to do that! It might be a better way to go than the workshop we were planning.

I look forward to your help in searching out what God wants me to do. How much does he want me to do? And what does he want me to refrain from doing? I do want to continue working in ways I can manage if possible.

I enjoy the opportunity to speak about the things I'm passionate about. But I also know that my ability to commit to things is very difficult. What a quandary!! If only I could lead a more stable life!

On the weekend, a lady from New Beginnings, an inner-city church at Hastings and Commercial asked if I could talk to their ladies' group. They do a lot of outreach and there is a lot of mental illness in their area. I'd love to speak to them and immediately said yes. I just hope she arranges to have me at a time I'm doing well. How good it would be to have a Living Room group in a church like that!

I thank God for the strength he gave me for the weekend and for how my mood is presently elevated. I can never take that for granted.

My prayer is for opportunity, strength, and stability.

With gratitude I pray.

CHAPTER SEVENTEEN

NEW STABILITY
2012

RETURN TO LEADERSHIP

February 9, 2012

My new psychiatrist got me started on Lithium and things began to look much better. I prayed:

"Thank you, God, for this new hope you've given me. So good to think that perhaps I'm going to be able to count on being well more often than I have been. What a gift that would be! I would be able to do more work for you. I would be stronger.

"Oh Lord, I pray for this. Give me your strength. Allow me to be an instrument for you in the best way possible. God, thank you for this reason to hope. Thank you for the scientists who discovered medications to help us live a better life.

'The Lord is my strength and my shield; my heart trusts in him, and I am helped. My heart leaps for joy and I will give thanks to him in song.' (Psalm 28:7)

"What a blessing it is when I trust you and find peace. How joyous I then find myself to be! I'm better able to notice and appreciate the garden—the flowers, the birds. If I could only always find it in me to trust you like that! To remember that you are my strength and that all good things come from you.

"And, in the way you always make the daisies grow each spring, you will be there for me.

'But those who wait for the Lord [who expect, look for, and hope in him] shall change and renew their strength and power; they shall lift their wings and mount up [close to

God] as eagles [mount up to the sun]; they shall run and not be weary, they shall walk and not faint or become tired.' (Isaiah 40:31 AMP)

"Lord God, that promise so speaks to me! My hope is in you in a big way, and how strong that makes me feel! I feel you healing me, strengthening me, making me better able to work for you. For so long I struggled with my health, hardly able to look after myself, needing so much help. But new medications are changing that. Thank you, Lord, for modern medicine. You have renewed my hope. And what a wonderful thing it is to have hope. New possibilities of serving you as a stronger person."

In Ephesians 2:10 Paul wrote:

"For we are God's workmanship, created in Christ Jesus to do good works, which God prepared in advance for us to do."

How encouraging that is! Does that mean that the limitations I have been worrying so much about should not hold me back so much after all? Hope for my future has greatly increased. Thank God for helping scientists come up with medications to help people with bipolar disorder! We are indeed fortunate to be living in this day and age.

February 18, 2012

I've been enjoying Erwin McManus's *Chasing Daylight: Seize the Power of Every Moment.* Although it's my third time reading this book, it still inspires me in the same way. McManus writes that life is an adventure which "comes at great risk and at significant cost. And life as God intends for you to live is nothing less than an adventure."

This book is hitting home so well for me right now as I'm gradually hoping to become more fully engaged in Living Room work again. A while back it was thought that I should avoid all big stressors and try to keep myself safe from excessive mood problems. But my new medication is working. I have regained the stability I lost.

"Thank you, God, for medicine! No need to continue playing it too safe."

Erwin McManus also wrote: "This is about stepping up and making sure life counts. It's about volunteering when God is asking, 'Who will go on my behalf?' I'm talking about our silent abdication of responsibility, our choice to move to the backdrop when someone is needed on the forefront."

"Yes, Lord, to keep playing it safe now that I'm more stable would indeed be abdicating my responsibility. What kind of life would I have playing it safe all the time? Life is an adventure and I'll need to live it, even if it means getting overwhelmed once in a while. God, I need to trust you again, as I trusted you from the beginning of Living Room.

"Yes I trusted, but you know how I faltered a lot too, Lord. There was a lot of fear. But you never failed to bring me back to the realization that I don't have to do the work alone. In fact, it's mostly you doing the work. All I have to do is to be a foot soldier for you. I just do what I'm told, taking advantage of opportunities that you provide, responding to those delicious urges to write that come from you. I want to be a voice for you, Lord."

I know that our God is very much present in all of Living Room's work. Through it, Christians living with mood disorders are able to be more open about themselves. With the help of God, they can deal with their emotional problems in an accepting and loving environment. It *is* a worthy adventure.

NEW MEDICATION AND TREMORS

March 9, 2012

I'm delighted. I've stabilized well. No sign of depression or mania. I feel that I can apply myself wholeheartedly again to my Living Room work.

But . . . and this is a big but . . .

My tremors are horrible. Jerky. Day before yesterday I dropped a glass in the bathroom sink when I was getting a drink of water. When I picked it up, I dropped it again. I dropped dishes when I was filling the dishwasher. I can't hang onto the soap when I take a shower.

I've had to give up on writing in my journal but am now using a laptop. I can use it in my favorite posture, sitting in my leather chair with my feet up. I hit a lot of wrong keys as I am writing this, but I'm always able to correct things.

Fortunately, the tremors ease up later in the day. They're at their worst in the morning.

The frustrating thing is that my psychiatrist doesn't seem to be considering this a serious problem. He's blaming all kinds of things. Other meds. My age. But not the Lithium. Yet it's when I started taking the Lithium that these severe tremors started.

I wish he would hear me! I wish he would treat me with more respect!

But we have Living Room today. Time to turn my thoughts to

positive things. One of our talented members will be leading the meeting using some songs she wrote. I'm looking forward to it.

A few months later, on July 7, 2012, I wrote:

> The uppermost thing on my mind right now is the tremors I've had since I started Lithium. I've had tremors for years. Maybe essential tremors; maybe because of meds. But five months ago, when I started Lithium, the tremors became so pronounced that it's hard to write or to photograph children, both activities that are such an important part of my life.
>
> A couple of weeks ago I was pouring boiling water into a carafe and I had one of the jerky tremors I often have and poured the water on my wrist instead. It created a nasty burn. My legs are affected as well. Last week I was trying to help some people out carrying things down a flight of stairs. I had to give up because I almost fell several times. I just could not do those stairs without hanging onto the banister. I have a hard time doing the circuit at the gym, because changing machines is such a clumsy ordeal for me. I feel like I'm becoming a cripple.
>
> I'm preparing to do some entertaining and the stress of it is increasing the tremors. How am I going to manage slicing the fruit to decorate the frozen cheesecake I'm making? Or chop the broccoli? I just got some new sharp knives and now I am afraid to use them. I'll have to ask for my husband's help. Yet I know he's getting tired of me becoming more and more dependent on him.
>
> Speaking engagements can be embarrassing as well. People think I'm looking awfully nervous and that's embarrassing. As a result, I get more nervous than I would otherwise.

Yet the Lithium has kept my mood so beautifully stable since I started taking it. What if I came off it and were to go on a less effective drug? What if I were to return to the rapid cycling I was experiencing before I went on it? No way would I want to go back there.

Should I just accept this and live with it or go on beta blockers—yet another medication? I recently read Michael J. Fox's story. He's a lot worse off than me. Yet look at how well he accepts it. Am I complaining too much?

POSTSCRIPT, written in 2024:
Lithium has been proven to stabilize people with bipolar disorder. However, for some it will cause tremors and other physical side effects, as it did for me. In the end, I developed ataxia, a degenerative disease causing lack of co-ordination. It meant that I eventually needed to use a walker to guard against falling. In writing about this, I recognize that these problems may not cause others to have the same side effects as I've had from this medication. For individuals taking Lithium, I would strongly recommend checking with a neurologist if tremors become a problem.

FINDING JOY

April 7, 2012 – to my blogging pals

This morning I was thinking how wrong it is that I think so much about depression and suffering. That's all I seem to have written about lately. It would be so much healthier to think and write about joyful things.

Good Friday was truly "good" for me. Our pastor had us focus on all the things I've been meditating on lately. His prayers helped me come to terms and talk to God about them.

But now it's time to think of Easter and the resurrection. It's time to focus on joy. The daffodils are blooming outside and the sun is shining beautifully. Time to start writing about happier things.

I wonder if I'm even capable of that? Writing about joy is something I haven't done for a long while. Yet I must try. For my mental health's sake, I must try.

I thought of a verse from the Psalms that has always meant a lot to me. *"This is the day the Lord has made. Let us rejoice and be glad in it."* (Psalm 118:24) Perfect to focus on at Easter time.

At the same time, I thought of an activity that brings me more joy than almost anything. I *love* marrying my photographs with favorite Bible verses, making bookmarks with them, and then sharing them with others. Two of my favorite things coming together: photography and Scripture.

So . . . I've made bookmarks to celebrate Easter. We will put one in each of the bulletins at church tomorrow. In every way a source of joy for me. And I hope for others as well.

My prayer:

"Father, thank you for the joy you gave me this morning creating this bookmark, one of my favorite Bible verses with one of my favorite photographs. And my pastor said I could share it with everyone tomorrow. I'm delighted.

"Lord, I wonder if Living room is always good for me? I'm so connected to it. Always thinking about depression. Personally, I've overcome my tough times, at least for a

while. And yet my thoughts are still so often wrapped up in these conditions.

"People come to me for help, looking for support. Many need to be protected from cruel stigma. I educate as much as I can through writing. This has become my life. It's the life you've given me. It's how I serve.

"It occurs to me how little I write about joy. There's something wrong here, Lord, that can't be healthy. You conquered death, and I shouldn't have to concern myself with it so much."

On April 12, 2012, I prayed:

"Father, where does this joy come from anyway? I know when I have it and often long for it, but can I willingly make myself joyful?

"I've been thinking lately about how I'm concerned so much with emotional pain and suffering. Not just my own but other people's too. Is that healthy, Lord?

"Yet the Bible says,

'Be joyful always; pray continually; give thanks in all circumstances, for this is God's will for you in Christ Jesus.' (1 Thessalonians 5: 16-18)

"How can I thank you when someone I support is feeling black and sees no way out? How can I feel joy then?

"Actually, when I pray and come into your presence with such a person, reminding her of how you are there and how you understand her pain, I feel compassion. When I assure her that your arms are there for her, and when this prayer gives comfort, that gives me joy. Lord, I feel you with us

then and I'm at peace. It's not a depressing thing at all to help a person in this way.

"Yes, God, we can find joy in the midst of suffering. I can see that now.

"But does the person who suffers—the person on the receiving end of my support—find joy as well? And you know, Lord, how often I am that person. Pretty hard to find joy then. And it's pretty hard to find someone who will pray with me in that way.

"Joy is to sit on the patio with the sun shining down on me. I feel joy when I focus my camera on a perfect grouping of Icelandic poppies and when I photograph them with thoughts of gratitude. Or when I see the early morning sunshine on the daisies making them dazzle.

"Thank you, God. It's contentment, I feel. It's a sense of peace filling me. Thank you for wellness, Lord, thank you for my present ability to feel joy."

April 30, 2012

"Lord, I feel like I've been arguing with you and I don't feel very good about it. I set out to find your truth and all I did was look for loopholes. I wasn't open to listening.

"Ever since I started following you I have found you and your Word trustworthy. You have helped me so much. When I've been stable, but even more so when I've been in trouble. Forgive me, God, for throwing so many questions filled with doubt your way.

"I want to focus instead on the tree you talk about in Jeremiah 17. How much more uplifting it would be to talk about that tree!

"This is what you told us in verses 5-8:

> *'Cursed is the one who trusts in man,*
> *who draws strength from mere flesh*
> *and whose heart turns away from the Lord.*
> *That person will be like a bush in the wastelands;*
> *they will not see prosperity when it comes.*
> *They will dwell in the parched places of the desert,*
> *in a salt land where no one lives.*
> *"But blessed is the one who trusts in the Lord,*
> *whose confidence is in him.*
> *They will be like a tree planted by the water*
> *that sends out its roots by the stream.*
> *It does not fear when heat comes;*
> *its leaves are always green.*
> *It has no worries in a year of drought*
> *and never fails to bear fruit.'*

"That fruit in the last verse reminds me of the fruit my friend talked about. The fruit of joy we experience when we stay connected to you. The fruit we have when we keep trusting you. You promise we will be like that tree, planted by the river, its roots easily reaching down to water. Even in years of drought, we will stay alive and produce fruit in season.

". . . and now I need to question you again, Lord: What about the long depressions some of us go through that last several seasons? When it really seems impossible to produce fruit? When we even start wondering why we're living? Some of us never escape the illness. Will our roots be able to keep drinking from the water where they're planted? Will you help us find reminders of your presence?

"I believe you will, Lord, with others' help. If we can reach out to godly friends maybe they will help keep our roots planted by the river. Trouble is, I know that many

depressed people who follow you, don't have friends like that who will be understanding and compassionate. That's the tough thing.

"My pastor quoted Gordon Fee yesterday during his sermon: "Joy does not mean the absence of sorrow but the capacity to rejoice in the midst of it." We can have that capacity if we keep trusting in you, like trees firmly planted by the river.

"That reminds me of David as we see him in the Psalms. In many of his writings he is obviously having a hard time and yet, in most cases he ends by rejoicing in God.

"If all of us could only be like David!"

GOD AT WORK IN LIVES

July 13, 2012

"Lord, I'm happy—so thankful about Living Room today. 22 people came, and you were there!!

"A., the Muslim woman, broke her silence and started asking many questions about God and about Jesus. She had been with us for quite a while seemingly afraid even to give her name. All five of us in our breakout group had a wonderful discussion with her.

"Poor girl! She thought that she was sick because she was being punished for things she had done wrong. We assured her that God is a God of grace.

"Lord, I pray that A. will learn to accept your gift of grace. I'm sure you're already at work in her life. Please help her welcome you in.

"I went to bed happy last night, thankful and at peace. Especially happy about A. Please lead me, God, in what I should do next. I need to remember that you save. You convert. It's not up to me.

"And so, I pray for her. I pray that she will come to fully know you and accept what Jesus did for her. Please help me share your love with her.

"Lord, I thank you for the many good things I see happening—the way you are working in Living Room people's lives. I thank you for the beautiful life you've given me.

"I feel led to use Matthew 11:28-30 for next Living Room's devotional. "Come to me all you who are weary and heavy laden and I will give you rest."

"Heavy laden with fears and worries and stress. Heavy laden with the effects of anxiety and depression. Lord, help me pull all the meaning out of this Scripture. Through it, minister to the members, especially A.

'Ask and it will be given to you; seek and you will find; knock and the door will be opened to you. For everyone who asks receives; he who seeks finds; and to him who knocks the door will be opened.' (Matthew 7:7-8)'"

August 19, 2012

"Lord, I'm looking at what's happening to our Living

Room membership and all of a sudden I realize what a mixture of people we're starting to serve.

"Not only do we have a big variety of disorders represented, but now we have a number of different faith traditions as well. We have Catholics, a Muslim, and now a Greek orthodox. And at the next meeting we'll have a Jewish person who wants to see how we do things. She wants to start a Jewish support group.

"It's really kind of overwhelming, God. I'll have to rely heavily on you for guidance so that I can serve them all well. Each person there needs to be encouraged to trust you, reminded of your never-ending love, even in hard times.

"Please help me plan something that will encourage and comfort the Muslim woman who has drawn so close to you. What great things you are doing for her, Lord! At the last meeting she opened up in an amazing way, talking about you and what you are doing for her. Even quoting parts of what you said, "Seek and you shall find." I was overjoyed to hear that. She repeated a prayer I said, accepting you into her heart. However, when I talked to her later, she wasn't so sure she had really and truly accepted you. She did tell me that the group had really helped her.

"Now we will have a Greek Orthodox woman joining us. I know her faith tradition is quite different from my evangelical Christian one. Will you help me speak into her life too, Lord? I have heard though, and I agree, that if I'm going to love and respect a person of another religion, I should be interested in their faith. I want to learn and understand what her faith is like.

"I certainly don't believe I should make it my business to change people's religion. Neither do I think I should make concessions for the various faiths represented in the group. I *need to be true to what I believe. I can only represent you in the way I know you to be. For me, it's all about honesty. Above all, each of us at Living Room needs to be honest: about our struggles, feelings, thoughts, and beliefs. We need always to be reminded that we are free to express what is inside us.*

"Living room is a place where we should be accepted, no matter where we are emotionally or spiritually. It's what you modeled for us when you did your ministry. You befriended and healed so many—whomever they were, wherever they were from.

"You accepted and loved them all. And if I'm going to follow you, and if Living Room is going to represent you, we need to strive to do the same. The message I need to pass along to my group is the message that you gave to those who came to you for love and for healing at the time you walked the Earth. Please help me to follow you, Lord."

AN ACTIVIST

April 19, 2012

Dear God,

"I don't like myself very much right now. Who do I think I am anyway, making such a big deal over something my pastor said? Am I actually cut out to be an activist?

"Somehow I don't think all this disagreeing and fussing over things makes me a very attractive person. Why can't I just be sweet and easy to get along with? I worry that some people are getting tired of me. What a nuisance I am! I'm embarrassed but can't seem to change. My pastor is one of the only people I can talk to about spiritual things.

"I'm not the quiet and submissive person I used to be—a person who doesn't get too upset about things. Respectful. What happened, God? Is the person I am today the person you intended me to be? I've changed so much from what I once was!

"Looking back, I can see I became a different person 25 years ago when I decided I couldn't do life on my own anymore. I made you part of my life. That's when all the changes started to happen. It's all your doing. Amazing all the things that have happened!

"Lord, without you I would not have had the courage to start my writing career with Sick, But No One Brought Me Flowers *for the Vancouver Sun. In one fell swoop everyone in my church, everyone who knew me, learned that I had spent time in a mental hospital. You made it possible for me to start writing honestly about things that people had for far too long kept silent. You took away my fears. You made me the teacher I always wanted to be, educating the public about mental health.

"In you I found someone I could trust and lean on when things got tough. I had always been unsure of myself. Shy. But you made me into a leader. How encouraging it is now, during times when I'm down, if I can remember that I don't live for myself alone.

"I became healthier. I don't remember too many psychotic episodes since that time. Of course, that's largely due to improved medications too. But didn't you make those possible as well?

"I thank you, God, for all you are. I thank you for your boundless love. I thank you for giving me a life worth living. It's really you who are doing all this work I'm part of now. It's not me at all. I'm only your instrument—your

pen, your voice, your hands, and feet. And I hope I have a
bit of your heart in me too. How can we work for you
without your heart?

"Maybe I should not dislike myself so much. You, God,
made me into the person I am. I guess it's okay to get angry
about injustices. You do that too. It's probably okay to
disagree with my pastor once in a while. Maybe I should be
proud to be an activist. Wasn't your Son one too?"

CHAPTER EIGHTEEN

THE CHILD IN ME
2012 -2013

A CHILD OF GOD

You may have noticed how I come across as a bit of a child through much of my story. And I do feel like a child in many ways.

You might be seeing it in how enthusiastic I am about Jesus. You might be seeing it in how vulnerable I am in my writings. I try to express my feelings and thoughts as clearly as possible. I try to openly show what's inside my heart. I guess I like having the spirit of a child in me because I've always liked children, even becoming a child photographer.

You might have seen the child in me come out in the eager way I told the people at Sacred Space about what it had meant for me to come to Jesus when I needed him so badly. I didn't hold anything back when I talked about what Jesus meant to me and how he helped me with my mental health issues. It was natural for me to do so. I can't help being a witness for Jesus. I can't help being true to my heart.

This is the way it was in all my speaking and writing when I raised mental health awareness in the Church and as I tried to help Christians learn what God can do in a life with mental illness. It shows in how freely I spoke as I was trying to explain how one can be a good Christian and still have a mental illness.

I'm not able to speak anything but the truth as I see it, feeling that injustice must be addressed. And in many cases I expose what I see to be unjust, no matter the harm that might come to me as a result. The world might call that courage . . . but I suppose some might think it a lack of wisdom. (typical of a child?)

I trust people too easily, perhaps putting them on a pedestal before I thoroughly know them. There have been times that I've become too attached to those who give the insecure child in me the attention I craved. This has caused problems for those who were trying to be kind to me.

I've had to be told by a caring person that it's only God who can be trusted. And that God can *always* be trusted.

Many think that being like a child means that one is immature, a person to be looked down on, lacking in wisdom. Many feel it's cause for shame. And yes, that's the world's point of view and often justifiably so. But Jesus thought differently. He told his disciples,

> *"Let the little children come to me, and do not hinder them, for the kingdom of God belongs to such as these. Truly I tell you, anyone who will not receive the kingdom of God like a little child will never enter it."* (Mark 10:14-15)

He must have said that because children's hearts are wide open. Many have a natural intimacy with God. The trouble for many grownups is that they know God in their heads but are not open enough to experience him in their hearts. Many try to find faith and gather wisdom from the books they read.

When they try to learn it all from books, there's a danger of losing their child-like heart of simplicity. Not that reading is bad, but it's not good to read books and use them to find a formula for developing faith. The simple faith of a child pleases God more than knowledge and wisdom learned in books.

Jesus said,

> *"I praise you, Father, Lord of heaven and earth, because you have hidden these things from the wise and learned and revealed them to little children."* (Matthew 11:25)

Do you remember what it was like to be a child?

Looking back at my own childhood, I recall feelings that were much more intense than those I have today as an adult. I loved my friends and family more deeply. The excitement that built as a birthday or Christmas approached knew no bounds. Joy made me bubble over. I remember the wonder and the innocence. I also remember times of vulnerability, acute pain, and fear. Occasionally all this resurfaces as I experience the ups and downs of life.

We are God's children, dearly loved by him. He wants to connect with us. This is what I hear him saying:

Open your hearts wide to receive the love I give you. Joyfully share that love with others. Wonder at the world I've made. Be amazed. Be wholehearted in what you do. Take your Bible—my Word—and receive what it says as my message to you, eagerly accepting it as truth. This is the child-like spirit I want to see in you.

I'd like to share the following devotional with you, written in May 2017. I felt a bit like the Mary in this story and wrote it from her point of view.

AT HIS FEET

As Jesus and his disciples were on their way, he came to a village where a woman named Martha opened her home to him. She had a sister called Mary, who sat at the Lord's feet listening to what he said. (Luke 10:38-39)

I've been hungry for more of Jesus. I'm eager to worship him. Wishing I could be like an enthusiastic child again as I was when I first wrote this piece.

Like Mary.

Why was Mary so eager to hear Jesus? What made him so special?

Jesus had wonderful lessons, many stories, and a love inside him that he freely shared. In those days women were discouraged from learning. For Mary to sit closer to Jesus than his disciples and men from the community was unheard of. Yet Jesus welcomed her. She was important to him.

Although her sister had complained that she wasn't helping with the housework, Jesus encouraged Mary to stay and listen to him. He told Martha, *"Mary has chosen what is better, and it will not be taken away from her."* In other words, he did not want her to be deprived of anything as special as the spiritual food he was offering.

This teacher was different from any other person she had known. He spoke in a way she hadn't heard before. He was wise, though humble. He revealed truth to Mary's hungry heart. By current standards, he was a radical, showing compassion for the sick and befriending those who were considered outcasts. He spoke about a heavenly kingdom, one that she would not have to wait for, but one that had already arrived.

When I read about Mary, I see her as someone who had a child's heart within her. The abundant enthusiasm and openness she had for learning was very much like that of a youngster.

Does Mary remind you of yourself—today, or as you once were?

The place Mary found at Jesus' feet is available to all of us. It's a place of comfort where you can be yourself, completely known and loved. It's a place where you'll be sure to find intimate friendship and spiritual rest.

ANXIETY FROM CHILDHOOD TRAUMA

October 25, 2012

I struggle all too often with an anxiety that I know stems from my childhood. When a friend I rely on for support has to go away, I panic. "What am I going to do without her?" This problem is not nearly as bad as it was. It seems to crop up most when I'm going through a period of depression.

This is a fear of abandonment, a terrible feeling that makes me feel like a child all over again. I believe this is the result of the many times I had to leave home before I reached the age of ten. I was often sick and in hospital. In the mid-forties and fifties parents were not allowed to visit, except for brief periods now and then. Being a shy and anxious child, these were hard times for me. I was also frequently sent away to stay with family or friends when my mother was sick.

And I clearly remember, when I was seven, eight, and nine years old, being sent away to a health camp for malnourished children. During my six weeks there, parents were only allowed to visit once, half-way through our time there. It's only in the past few years that I have recognized how traumatic my childhood actually was and how it's affecting me today, at 66.

Yesterday I was feeling that anxiety and I wondered: should I feel compassion for the little child that is still inside me, or would that be feeling sorry for myself? And should I then be forgiving myself for feeling that way? But I didn't do anything wrong, did I? And yet I feel ashamed.

A friend who also suffered during childhood and is having trouble with her mental health because of it, told me, "No. It's fine to feel compassion for yourself. It doesn't mean you're necessarily feeling sorry for yourself at all. It only means that you should be kind and gentle with yourself."

S

Thinking of it that way comforts me. We need to comfort ourselves. We need to allow God to comfort us.

And as my thoughts progressed yesterday, I realized that I have compassion for people at Living Room who struggle with anxiety. I can see that the things I'm going through right now are going to help me better understand their pain. And when I have compassion for others, am I not indirectly having compas-sion for myself as well?

I'm thinking of Jesus now and how he loves us. He has compassion for us. He loves the part of us that still hurts like a little child and he will comfort that child.

I believe that trusting God in this way will go a long way to healing our anxiety.

MISSIONS FEST, 2013

January 2013

Our presence at Missions Fest in 2013 was once more a tiring but wonderful experience. I started making note of all the contacts we were making with visitors to our booth but had to give up. There were far too many. I was only able to make note of a few:

On Friday, before opening, someone walked by saying, "We

love you guys." A few minutes later, a couple passed by. The lady wanted to know what caused mood disorders—why the prevalence? The husband worked for Coast and knew my psychiatrist. She is going to put our brochure in her album and pray for me.

One person spent a lot of time talking, bought a book, and prayed for me. Meantime, a lady passing by said, "It's high time." Half an hour later, a couple spent some time with us, bought manuals, and told us about a depressed friend in Maple Ridge.

Once again, people expressed a need for a group in Surrey. I prayed that an opportunity would materialize. I saw a need to write a letter, persuading churches there and elsewhere to start a group. This was something I soon did.

We certainly *needed* to be at Missions Fest. With one in five experiencing mental health issues, of course many people stopping at our booth were very happy to see what we had to offer. By being there we were cutting through the stigma, giving people an opportunity to talk about mental health in a Christian setting.

I felt privileged—blessed—to be included in this good work that God was doing.

> *"Lord, I'm going to have so much follow-up work to do. Such a lot of work to go over. Help me to do each piece of work calmly, unrushed, thoughtfully. Help me please to enjoy the work and not feel overwhelmed. Be in all I do because this is your work and not my own. I love serving you in this ministry."*

But now I need to rest.

DEVOTIONALS

In mid-February 2013, I invited all my contacts to join my list of people to whom I would be sending devotionals via Mailchimp. I started doing this out of concern for the many who did not have access to a Living Room group but needed the spiritual support. This email ministry became an extension of the Living Room ministry, one that I continue serving today in 2024.

Although I went through some very bad times, God helped me keep on writing and sharing in this way. And sometimes it was during my greatest struggles that I was able to do the most helpful writings. I've always said that it was very much the Holy Spirit that helped me at such times. I felt closest to Jesus when I suffered, and believe I was then best able to help readers come close to him as well.

When I started writing and sending out my Mailchimp devotionals, reading and writing became hugely important to me, more so it seems than planting more groups.

I started focussing more on enriching the spiritual needs of people with mood disorders—both for individuals who couldn't make it to Living Room meetings, as well as for the new Living Room groups for whom I wrote interactive devotionals.

I prayed:

> *"Dear God, I so love writing my inspirational devotionals for people living with mood disorders. Please remain with me as I write. Please help me keep the writing fresh and good. Help my writings encourage people to help them cope. Help me stay close to you.*

"I was happy about the response to my emails. One came that was especially touching. I knew that this kind of reaction could only come in response to words coming from you, Lord. Thank you for letting me join with you in your work. Such blessings it brings me."

Through my writings I carried the spirit of Living Room onward to reach beyond the meetings that were forming. There would never be enough groups to meet the needs of the many who were struggling. But writings could be published and enjoyed by many.

There are now 230 devotionals for personal use available to download off my website and 60 interactive devotionals for group use. They can be accessed by going to https://marjabergen.com/devotionals.

CRESST TREATMENT CENTER

In the fall of 2013, I was admitted to CRESST, a ten-bed psychiatric facility, to determine whether my abnormal sleep pattern and religious fervor were related.

I'm not sure of this, but I believe that by that time, I was going to bed around 8 pm, sleeping for 5 hours, getting up at 1:00 or 2:00 am, until I lay down around 5 am for a nap. In the intervening time, I spent time with God—reading my Bible or nonfiction books, journalling, and writing devotionals to send out to a list of people. For a period of time, I also used this time to develop interactive devotionals to share with Living Room groups. If I got tired during the day, I simply lay down for a nap. I still follow that sleep pattern as I'm writing this in 2024.

My husband and psychiatrist complained, thinking this abnormal and wanting me to change my habits. But the quiet hours this gave me with Jesus were rich and precious. I was aware that my behavior wasn't normal but had tried repeatedly to have better and longer sleeps, finding it impossible.

My strong spirituality caused my case manager and psychiatrist concern. I considered having my counselor at the time write a note to them to explain the importance of my faith life. This is what it means for me to walk close to God. But it's hard for non-Christians to understand.

I didn't really think I needed to be here, but it did feel good to be taken care of. I had been under a lot of stress, trying to do far more than I should—feeling pressure from many sources to do more.

This treatment center, though not perfect, was my refuge for just over three weeks and I was glad for it. For the first while I spent a lot of time writing, happy to have that freedom. I had more opportunities to write here than I did at home. How grateful I was for that!

A few days after arriving at CRESST, a nurse told me that I had to stop talking so much to other residents. She said that I'm there for my own health. I needed to think more about myself and less about others. I ended up in tears.

After that I tried to stick to myself, but people kept coming to me, telling their stories. Mostly all I did was listen. My journal does show that at one point I prayed,

> *"Lord, I've met so many good believers here—and it's not because I went around making a big deal about believing in you. My belief in you just came oozing out with no effort."*

Everyone knew about it. Later I found out that word had gone around that I was a priest.

In the homey atmosphere of this small facility I had a chance to put my responsibilities aside for a while and come to rest. Medical staff worked to adjust my medications and closely monitored me to see how they were working.

Although this facility was not a Christian one, I did feel God's presence in a big way. It's amazing how people get in touch with their spirituality when they're in the midst of emotional crises. Amazing how much God came up in discussions with fellow residents.

I hope I'll always remember dear L. who bent over me when I was in tears and told me he'd pray for me. It hadn't occurred to me that he believed in God.

I'll remember S. the rough and tumble man with substance abuse problems and schizoaffective disorder, openly telling me about his life. He broke down and cried when he told me how badly he felt about the things he had done. He knew that God forgave him, but he couldn't forgive himself.

And I will fondly remember F. an Iranian man who told me, "I don't have a religion, but" —and touching his hand to his chest — "I have a special place in my heart for Jesus." We ended up in a wonderful discussion, talking about all the things we love about Jesus.

Would such discussions have so easily developed out in the "healthy" world? I've never known them to. And although I'm a very spiritual person, ready to share, I did not knowingly initiate any of this, nor the many others that took place. Where did they come from? How did God so magically appear in our conversations?

Being in psychiatric care wasn't so bad.

APPENDICES

THE IMMENSE VALUE OF PEER SUPPORT

It's wonderful how much work is being done to raise mental health awareness in the Church today. Looking back to the time when I started my work in the year 2000, there was so much ignorance that individuals with mental health issues were leaving their churches because of the hurt inflicted on them by fellow Christians who told them that there must be something wrong in their relationship with God. That, thank God, is happening a lot less today.

Christians and their churches have been learning about mental health—the various illnesses and how they present themselves in those who live with them. They learn to accept and support the individuals in their church who live with such challenges. They learn how to respond to their needs.

But have we asked such people about their needs? Have they had opportunities to tell us how the pain of stigma has affected them? Do they have people with similar problems with whom they can share their pain, so that they don't feel so alone with it?

There is something important left out of the teachings the Church has been receiving. And that is an understanding of what people with mental health challenges can do for each other—the support they can offer their peers. There is no support as effective as the kind of support people can give to those who share similar needs—those who understand what it's like to live with the problems they face in trying to live in this world. Those who need Jesus as he is shown in the gospel stories.

(Note the work done by researcher Phyllis Solomon, PhD, below.)

The most important way in which people with mental health challenges can support each other—better than anyone else can—is by helping each other find assurance in the great love God has for them and how he values them, despite the way the world treats them. Those who don't know what it is to have lives like they do could never understand that message in the same way.

Those who live with mental health challenges, need spiritual support that differs from messages most frequently delivered in churches. More than anything, they need to hear how a radical Jesus tried to change the status quo by showing the love of God to those the world was rejecting.

This is the picture of Jesus that people with mental health issues most need to see and hear. Knowing such a Jesus is their unique spiritual need. And this is the kind of need that Christians who want to be supportive need to address. When that understanding of the love of Jesus is taught—and shown as well by fellow Christians—healing will occur. This is what Jesus meant when he called us to follow him.

And yet, such an understanding of Jesus can be hard to fathom by those who are emotionally healthy—those who don't face rejection in the way people with mental health issues do. This picture of Jesus who was accepting, kind, and showed the love of God to the outcasts is best shared by those who, like us, are rejected by the world today.

I speak from a different perspective than what is usually heard. I speak as one who has needed support in her life with a major mental illness. I was—and still am—one who has, at the same time, spent 18 years of her life giving spiritual support to those living with such illnesses. I'm also one who was rejected in ways that would be unimaginable to those who have good mental health.

In other words, I understand the needs of people with mental health issues from three perspectives—as a giver and receiver of support, and as one who has suffered. I understand in a way few people do.

As founder of the faith-based Living Room support ministry which began in 2006, I have always believed in the importance of the support people with mental health issues can give each other. Unfortunately the Living Room ministry that at one time had 16 groups stretching across Canada, was disbanded in 2018. Only two or three small groups remain. It has been a great loss to those who need to know about God and his love for them.

In 2015, I spent a couple of weeks in hospital on a mental health ward, suffering deeply while alone in my room. But the moment I went into the lounge and started talking with fellow patients, the pain lifted as we talked about what had brought them into hospital. "What's your name? How are you doing?" I must have come across as someone who cared, because before long we were talking about spiritual things. And I don't believe I initiated it.

While in hospital I journaled the following:

> "Lord, this continues to be the most amazing place to meet people and see you at work. Your name so often comes up. Spirituality is a big topic of conversation here. People who have faith. People who wonder what God has to offer. People with strange beliefs—foggy beliefs—nothing certain."

Through my experiences as a patient in psychiatric facilities and my support of individuals in crisis, I have learned how great the hunger for God is. I recognize this in a way healthier supporters might not.

Although I was undergoing one of the most painful periods in my life, I experienced joy in the midst of it when I talked with others about God.

Why the joy?

It was because I was with others who had needs that were similar to mine. It was because we could explore what God might have to offer to fill those needs. It was the best kind of support we could have asked for—support from our peers. Doctors and nurses could not help us as much as we—through God—helped each other.

Being with others who share our needs is not always possible out in the community. The only place where such peer support could take place and our faith expressed, would be within a group of people where everyone has such needs. Together it becomes possible to discuss our needs with others who can relate. Such a place offers opportunities for us to explore Scripture and learn what it says to us in terms of living a life with mental health difficulties.

This shows the importance of groups designed specifically for the support of people with mental health challenges. Nothing can compare to individuals sharing the pain they all understand and expressing the kind of need for Jesus they all long for. And no Bible study compares to such people joining together in finding that need met in Scripture.

Christian peer support groups are vitally important. There are few other places where individuals with mental illness can gather to talk about both: their emotional struggles and their trust in God. Those who don't have lived experience can't hope to empathize in the way peers can.

Studies by researchers like Phyllis Solomon, have shown that peer support is more effective than support given by people who have never experienced such issues.

Phyllis Solomon, PhD is Professor in the School of Social Policy & Practice and Professor of Social Work in Psychiatry at the University of Pennsylvania. Her research has been on the forefront of consumer rights and capabilities, having conducted one of the first and most influential studies on consumer provided mental health services in the 1990s. ("consumer" was the term once used to describe a person with mental health challenges.)

Although rigorous empirical research was limited, she shows the following outcomes as promising: "They include increased self esteem, sense of control, empowerment, hope. belief in bringing about change in their lives, sense of belonging, social support, engagement in self management services, treatment, and community, and improved social functioning, quality of life and life satisfaction. Further, peer support also resulted in decreases in hospitalizations, self stigma, psychotic symptoms, depression, substance abuse, and fewer feelings of social isolation." (From Psychiatric Quarterly, 2022)

A CALL FROM GOD FOR US ALL

It was around the year 2000 when I initially received God's call to help Christians understand what it is to have a mental illness and to help them learn to accept and love those affected. I witnessed, telling them what God had done for me in my life with bipolar disorder. I wrote and spoke extensively about the importance of faith for all who suffer from mental health challenges. I described how God can work in the lives of people with such challenges.

In 2006, God led me to the founding of faith-based support groups called Living Room where people with such illnesses were able to gather with their peers, in a safe place sharing both—their faith and their mental health problems. Many had been shamed out of their churches, where they were all too often blamed for their own suffering—considered to be distant from God. Living Room gave them what their churches couldn't.

Living Room helped its participants see how God values them and loves them, no matter what. They found out how the love of Christ could bring healing to their emotional pain. They were able to share with their peers, learning that they weren't alone.

From the beginning, I recognized Living Room to be God's work, not mine. I was only his foot soldier. Other than that, I served alone as leader of this effort. From the beginning, I knew there needed to be others in place to follow me if anything were to happen to me. I now believe that God had more in mind.

I believe that ALL of us who want to follow Jesus are called by God to be part of Living Room, no matter who we are or where we live. Every one of us is called to do our part in giving spiritual support to those who are being rejected by the world. We are called to follow Christ's example.

From the year 2009, I felt that God intended Living Room to be a movement—one that shouldn't belong to anyone in particular—not a person, a church, or any organization. It was a concept that I wasn't at the time able to make understood by others. But it's clear to me today.

Living Room should live freely within the hearts of all those who love God and want to pass that love along to those who hunger for it.

Over the years, I have learned that Living Room is a lot more than just a group ministry. In 2013, I started writing devotionals, emailing them to people who might not have access to groups. It was, and still is, Living Room. Through those mailings, many have found encouragement for their faith journey and a healing of emotional pain.

Devotionals are sent out to over 200, twice a week—to all kinds of people, not only those who are struggling emotionally. These mailings continue today, over ten years later.

In the name of Jesus, we can all play a part in healing the painful effects of stigma in those who are rejected by the world. By looking at Jesus and seeing how he's portrayed in the gospels, we can follow the example he set for us 2000 years ago.

What is the essence of Living Room? (first written in my journal in 2009)

"The basis for the Living Room support model, the foundation on which it rests, is the love of Jesus Christ. Knowledge of his love, the depth of which we try but can never quite grasp, is what we believe is our key to wholeness. We learn to trust God, asking him to fill us with his love and to help us share that love with others. This is how we can bring healing to our lives and to the lives of others."

LIVING ROOM UPDATE

In July 2014, I gave up the Living Room ministry, no longer able to give it what it needed, relieved that it would be merging with Sanctuary Mental Health Ministries, hopeful it would have a better future with them. Tears of regret flowed over having to let it go. Living Room had been my calling, a vibrant ministry since 2006. But there had been no indication that help would be forthcoming. I felt guilty for not being able to continue.

Four years later, in 2018, I was crushed to hear Sanctuary's announcement that Living Room would no longer be part of their mandate. I did all I personally could to change their minds, but in effect the ministry drew to a halt. At the time of writing, only three small groups remain that I know of.

Since that time, I've been trying to be a voice for those who are no longer heard—the many with lived experience whose support was abandoned. I continue Living Room work by sending out Reflections on Scripture as I had been since 2013. These mailings are encouraging all who are on the list, reminding them of the love Jesus showed during his ministry on earth.

I still try to reduce stigma from the perspective of a person with lived experience, as I had since 1993. Through my writings I work to instill confidence in those living with low self-esteem. My passion is to do all I can to help people realize that the painful effects caused by stigma can be overcome through the healing love of Christ. As Christians, we are called to follow the radical unconditional love Christ showed us in the gospels.

On January 17th, 2010, I wrote about my dream of Living Room becoming a movement, in the way AA had become a movement, stretching far and wide. One thing I believe is that God would not want Living Room to be a ministry of a single person or group of persons, nor a ministry of any one particular church, nor a ministry belonging to an institution. The heart and soul of Living Room should move freely, wherever there are people with mental health needs, and wherever the unconditional love of Jesus Christ is taught.

> "I was reading a chapter in one of Max Lucado's books about "fear of dying." And it occurred to me how I wouldn't be afraid to die. But before I die, I want to build Living Room into something firm and strong." *"Oh God, how I would like to build something that carries on after I die."*

The words from Isaiah 28:16 came to mind: *"I am placing a foundation stone in Jerusalem. It is firm, a tested stone that is safe to build on."*

The tools for running a Living Room group are still available. I have the Facilitator's Manual, updated in 2023, and 60 interactive devotionals are on my website at https://marjabergen.com/devotionals. If requested, I could supply many writings on the topic of Living Room leadership. I hope that the enthusiasm I showed in this book will have rubbed off on some of you. Might you even be hearing the call to form a group of your own?

It would be wonderful if a passionate person would partner with one or two others and consider creating and hosting a website making all this information available for would-be facilitators of groups to download. Could peer support see the light of day once more?

Think about it. Pray about it. It's God's work.

If you'd like to talk, my email address is
marja@marjabergen.com.
My website is at https://marjabergen.com/

marja